About the Author

Craig V. Abbott II, lives in Central New York where he was born. He has Spinal Muscular Atrophy Type 1, is wheelchair bound, and has triumphed over every hurdle that has been thrown his way. He continues astonishing his doctors, family, and friends by beating the odds. *Blood and Lust* is his first solo project as well as his first fictional novel. He enjoys his time by reading, writing, playing poker, and taking walks with his Boxer/Pit named Lucy. He is currently working on the sequel for this series, and hopes to inspire readers and writers everywhere to pursue their dreams!

Blood and Lust:
The Insignificant Life of Rick Blume

Craig V. Abbott II

Blood and Lust:
The Insignificant Life of Rick Blume

Olympia Publishers
London

www.olympiapublishers.com
OLYMPIA HARDBACK EDITION

Copyright © Craig V. Abbott II 2022

The right of Craig V. Abbott II to be identified as author of this work has been asserted in accordance with sections 77 and 78 of the Copyright, Designs and Patents Act 1988.

All Rights Reserved

No reproduction, copy or transmission of this publication may be made without written permission.
No paragraph of this publication may be reproduced, copied or transmitted save with the written permission of the publisher, or in accordance with the provisions of the Copyright Act 1956 (as amended).

Any person who commits any unauthorised act in relation to this publication may be liable to criminal prosecution and civil claims for damage.

A CIP catalogue record for this title is available from the British Library.

ISBN: 978-1-80439-227-0

This is a work of fiction.
Names, characters, places and incidents originate from the writer's imagination. Any resemblance to actual persons, living or dead, is purely coincidental.

First Published in 2022

Olympia Publishers
Tallis House
2 Tallis Street
London
EC4Y 0AB

Printed in Great Britain

Dedication

For Nate V.B. — I wish that you could see how this all turned out, because I think you would have loved it. I miss you, friend — this one's for you.

Acknowledgements

First and foremost, I would like to thank my mom. She supports me in everything I do, and I wouldn't be where I am without her and her unfailing belief in my talents. (Thanks, Mom. I love you.) To RJS, who did an amazing job helping me bring my characters to life; I could not have written this without you. I am happy to call you my editor and friend, and can't wait to see what we do next. To Aaron Weiss, for the time and work he put into designing my website and helping me build my platform; I am grateful for, and indebted to, his enthusiasm as a webmaster. To Brenda Dann and her family, who have been amazing friends. Whether around the kitchen table or the poker table, Brenda is always helpful. I especially appreciate her photography skills, and how easy she is to work with. And finally, to my grandfather, Richard E. Wheeler. Every day I strive to be the man he saw in me, and I hope he'd be proud of who I've become (even though I know this book would not have been his cup of tea). I miss him every day.

Author's Note

This book depicts issues of death, violence, gore, sexual violence, and strong sexual content. It is my hope that these topics have been handled with sensitivity, but if these could be considered triggering to you, please be advised.

Chapter One

I sat at my usual table in Paul's Café while I took in the scent of the freshly-ground coffee beans. Everything about that Monday morning was routine for me, right down to the familiar smell of the blueberry muffins Maryanne had just pulled from the oven. I was half asleep, hungover, and definitely not ready for work. But there was no way I could afford to call in again — not on my paycheck. Besides, who else was going to pay for my drinking problem and recently-rediscovered gambling addiction?

God, I hate Mondays.

Paul's Café was small, but large enough for elbow-room between the few regular customers who camped there each day. I liked it that way as I preferred to keep to myself. Though I'd always wished I had more friends or was more inclined to be social, people didn't seem to like me very much. I tended to get nervous in any-sized crowd of people, and rejection — even from strangers — cut like a knife every time. You'd think I'd gotten used to it after a lifetime's worth, but no. There was nothing I feared more than getting rejected.

Fuck. My head is pounding.

My head was swimming from guilt, and gin. Not for the first time, I found myself wondering why in the hell did I do that to myself? Over and over again I wondered why I'd drank so much the night before. Every night, really. Even though I knew I would wake up with no energy and a severe, booze-induced headache, I just couldn't seem to put the bottle down. But at that point I didn't see any good reason to stop drinking, as nothing was really going for me in life. As sad as it was to admit, the alcohol was actually my best friend. Like a good companion, the gin kept me relaxed and sleepy, and helped me not to care that I led such an empty life.

I knew I should have stopped after the first few G&Ts last night... But knowing and doing... knowing and doing. Plus, my mother didn't raise no quitter.

My head throbbed with each passing second as I waited for the clock to tell me that it was time to go to work. Hoping that the clock on the wall was wrong somehow, I pulled my cell phone from my jeans pocket and tapped on the screen to light it up.

Damn. 8:37 a.m. Well, congrats on being annoyingly accurate, clock.

After confirming that I only had a few minutes before I needed to leave, I shoved my phone in my pocket and turned my attention back to the window. The overhead light glinted off the lenses of my glasses as I turned my head, which generated a fleeting white flash that bounced from my glasses, to the plate-glass window, and back to my bloodshot eyeballs. I winced and groaned as the bright light punched through my hangover and pierced my brain.

Instead of focusing on the reflection of my groaning, bespectacled thirty-six-year-old self in the glass, I watched the exciting bustle of New York City through the large oval windows that looked out to the street in front of Paul's Café. The wind was beginning to pick up and the skies were spitting tiny droplets of rain. Typical for that time of year, really. The fall in New York always brought rain and damp. At least it wasn't that frozen white stuff. I dreaded the snow and winter, but the end of fall signaled they were coming. Soon.

I watched multiple leaves of varying colors fall to the ground, one by one. First a yellow one, then orange. A red leaf landed briefly on the jacketed shoulder of a woman before she brushed it off impatiently. Then, a light brown leaf was whipped against the window where it slowly slid down the glass, leaving a trail of water trickles behind it.

Yeah, I understand — I'm just as useless as you are. The boring life of the insignificant Rick Blume... Stupid leaf.

I leaned forward and gently flicked the glass with two fingers, causing the leaf to fall and land in a small puddle on the sidewalk. An old man wearing a black suit and hat came along and picked up the leaf with the bottom of his shoe. It stuck, they were off and on their way to who knew where.

That damned leaf was gonna have more excitement today than I was. How pathetic.

I sat back down and was about to finish nursing my black coffee, which had gone cold during my window-gazing, when I noticed something different about that otherwise routine, dreary morning. Her. She was absolutely gorgeous. She was attractive and petite — she couldn't have been more than five-foot-two, standing against the counter as she waited for her order. She had long, blonde hair that cascaded down her back past her voluptuous, perfectly-rounded backside. She turned to her left to reach for a sugar packet, and her profile revealed the perkiest set of breasts I had ever seen — not too large, probably a nice, full C-cup. Just enough to fit in your hands — or your mouth, if you were lucky. Then I saw her lips, and that smile. Her smile could have lit up a room. She looked young and innocent, but something in her smile told me she was mature and experienced. I was more than a little intrigued by this mystery woman, whose skin and posture were as flawless as the tight red dress she was wearing. Not a rip or wrinkle in sight. The tops of her breasts were practically spilling from the neckline of the dress. I pictured her naked as she tapped sugar from its packet into her waiting coffee. Seeing her brought new meaning to the word 'perfection'.

I blinked a few times to make sure she was real. And she definitely was. I was used to seeing older people or married couples with children in Paul's, but never beautiful creatures like her.

I wonder what she looks like out of the dress. Should I try to talk to her…? No. Don't be ridiculous, Rick, she probably wouldn't even acknowledge you. You're a fool. She's a goddess. And you're hungover.

I had never seen a woman so deeply alluring in all of my thirty-six years, let alone in Paul's Cafe. I knew just about everyone who walked through those oak-stained double doors and across the cafe's wooden floors, but no one ever like her. The only people in Paul's I didn't know, were the few one-off customers who would occasionally walk in off the street, so I thought I had a good handle on the type to gather at Paul's. After all, I'd been going there every morning before work for the last seven years. I was one of Paul's few regulars, and we numbered in the single digits — including Paul's employees.

Looks like you don't know everyone here, hot shot. Maryanne Prescott was the barista who took exactly sixty seconds to make you a caffeinated beverage, and then charge you three arms and a leg for it. Inflation, whatever. The cafe was literally on my way to work, so I was willing to foot the bill for convenient caffeine.

Maryanne was a sweet and gentle woman, with warmth in her brown eyes and matching long, brown hair which flowed past her shoulders. I considered her a beautiful person, inside and out. She was compassionate and loving, unless you made her angry. Then she got crazy, but I figured that's any woman — every woman. 'Hell hath no fury', like the saying goes. Or so I'd heard, at least — I had no experience with women, so I had to rely on what books, movies, and other people could tell me.

In the corner sat Christo Daggen, a fellow regular. Christo was an aging, balding, Italian loan shark who was always accompanied by his faithful toady. They always sat at the same table in the same corner of the café in matching leather jackets where Christo would chomp on the unlit cigar in his mouth. He was the one person in Paul's I was careful not to piss off. The people not as careful disappeared. Nobody ever seemed to question him or the strange occurrences that followed him and his lackey, and I wasn't about to rock the boat. *He must have serious connections. Like, make-people-disappear-and-get-away-with-it connections.*

Then there was the owner and manager. It was Paul's Cafe, and he was Paul — a hardworking, middle-aged man who seemed content eking out a living doing what he loved. Though the café opened fifteen years before, he looked like he hadn't aged a day — let alone enduring fifteen years of New York City living. Lucky bastard. Even though he wasn't making a ton of money in coffee and muffins, he was the role model for a regular guy living his regular dream. He was a tall man and usually kept a little bit of a stubble on his face, which completed the 'regular' look. He wore a blue sapphire necklace shaped like a triangle that he never took off, which struck me as out of place with the rest of his usual get-up. I never saw him without it. Jewelry notwithstanding, he was the boss around the café, and a decent enough guy. Whether you had a complaint, or a compliment, or a request for more homemade cinnamon raisin toast, you went to Paul.

After staring at her for what was probably an inappropriately long time, the mysterious blonde grabbed her coffee and promptly turned away from the counter. She made her way back to Christo and his goon in the corner of the café.

What the hell does she want with him? Does she want him to help her out with her finances, or something? Is he paying her to fuck him for the night? Is she a call girl? If she was a prostitute, she was definitely high-end. She was easily a thousand-dollar-a-night kind of girl, which Christo could have afforded no problem. I didn't have that kind of money, even though I would have loved to blow a whole week's paycheck on her, if not more. *Ten minutes. Just give me ten minutes with you. Really, I'm not greedy.*

Whatever her business with Christo was, it was a safe bet that it would be frowned upon by the government; everyone knew that Christo wasn't afraid of getting his hands dirty, which was ironic because he owned a dry-cleaning business. But everyone also knew that the business was a front. If you could get by the six-foot-three, three hundred pounds of a bouncer — Lazarus, Christo's lackey — there was a high-stakes poker game in the back room six nights out of seven. I used to go. A lot. Too much, really. It was an invitation-only game, and definitely not for beginners; I had seen people walk in there with thousands of dollars and walk out with nothing but a black eye or a broken shoulder.

Oh, maybe she's going to be the new topless dealer. I might actually get to see her naked. Hot damn! God. Who am I kidding? I'm never going to see her naked. Not in this lifetime, anyways. Wishful thinking, dumbass.

Christo and his thug sat with their backs to the wall as the woman walked over to stand directly in front of them. She leaned over their table, and all I could see was her ass. I wasn't complaining (!), but I was curious as to what she could possibly have to say to the shady pair. She whispered something in his ear while her hand rested on his shoulder. After she'd said whatever she needed to, she headed back to the counter to grab another coffee and a brown paper bag from Maryanne. Whatever conversation she'd had with Christo didn't take long, so I figured it was strictly business. Though I guess it could have been strictly pleasure.

Fuck. I really hope Christo doesn't get to have her. Damn. I was revulsed by the image of this gorgeous woman fucking the old gangster, but it kept playing in my head like a bad movie on an airplane. I couldn't shake the revolting idea, and I needed to go.

It was almost nine a.m., and I was stalling. I knew if I didn't get my ass moving, I'd be late for work. It would have been worth being late to get a chance to talk to the beautiful woman, new to Paul's Café. I took one last look at her and convinced myself I must be daydreaming, but a parting glance of the dream girl was all I had time for. As my eyes scanned her body, I caught her already staring at me. My green eyes locked onto her baby blues, and I couldn't look away. I would have spent my entire day staring at her, the most wonderful thing I had ever seen in my life.

Please don't get awkward. Please don't say anything to me. I tried to think about how to make our introduction less awkward, and what I could possibly say that didn't make me sound like a total stalker. *Hey, I'm the guy you caught freakishly watching you from across the room. Sorry I didn't have the courage to formally introduce myself but it's because I have no balls... Yikes.*

I got up from my table to settle up at the counter to pay, and then head out for work. I kept my head down and my eyes trained on the wooden floors as I walked to the register so that my staring wouldn't be so obvious to her, or Christo. The last thing I wanted was to make a scene, let alone irritate Christo. I paid Maryanne. I received her reliably congenial smile and wave along with my change. I tossed a generous tip into the sad jar on the counter like always, then grabbed my second coffee and blueberry muffin to go. I needed that second cup to take with me to work; coffee seemed to be the only thing getting me through the days. Well, coffee and the big bottle of gin that awaited me at home.

I pushed through the oak-stained double doors and stepped out onto the sidewalk to head to work. I was greeted by the rain, and wished I had checked the forecast for the day so I could have known to bring an umbrella, even though I'd spent the morning staring at the rain through the oval windows when not staring at the blonde.

As I walked, I made a promise I knew that I would never keep: I promised myself that if I ever saw the blonde again, I would grow the courage to approach her, and even attempt a conversation. I tried to summon confidence as I passed the reflective windows of each skyscraper, and while I waited for the traffic lights to give me permission to cross the bustling, New York City streets.

Rick, you're awesome: you have a job, a car, and an apartment. She'll love you, man! If she's not interested in Christo, you might actually have a shot. Every person I saw on the street reminded me of her. Woman or child, man or boy. It didn't make a difference. I saw her face in everyone who passed me.

Bullshit. It's a shitty job, a piece-of-junk car — which is why I'm walking to work — and the so-called apartment? Well, it has a roof, a bed, and a bathroom. Oh, but let's not forget that quality television that features a whopping eight channels, on a good day.

It was easy to make myself a promise when the chances I'd run into her again seemed extremely slim in a city of almost ten million souls. Part of me hoped that she would become a regular business partner for Christo so I could at least be able to look at her again. Even from a distance. But I also knew that any serious involvement with Christo meant I should stay as far away from her as I could. That was my general approach with Christo; steer clear. Except his poker game, which was the one thing I was actually good at. Though, I was only as good as luck allowed, which usually didn't amount to much.

As I walked, I thought I saw her in the windows of the buildings I passed. Instead of seeing my glasses, my bed-head brown hair, my wan cheeks and prominent nose reflected in the glass, it was her. She was looking at me, wearing the same red dress, waving me toward her, begging me close. I saw her again in the next building. She was on her knees with her head tipped back licking her thick lips, stained a blood-red almost identical to that of her dress. *Is she begging to put me in her* mouth? *That would be so awesome.*

I was getting hard just thinking about her putting her mouth on any part of me, but especially a few particular parts.

I saw her again in the window of the next building, and she was holding me. I was leaning back with the full length of my throat exposed to her. It looked like she wanted to bite into me. I seemed unable to move, and I looked frightened. I watched as she pushed her teeth against my neck to rip flesh and then drink my blood. All of it. She drained every ounce of life from me, drop by drop. I was watching her slowly kill me in the reflection. She looked up at me through the window while holding my lifeless body, and I saw how different she looked from the red-dressed vixen I'd seen in Paul's. Her face was full of wrinkles, especially in her brow. Her eyes were no longer blue, but red. She locked her bright red eyes onto mine as if she was staring straight through me. And her mouth — open and dripping with blood. My blood. It trickled from her lips and the tips of her fangs.

Fangs? Why does she have fangs? And what's with her eyes? Were they red this morning? I was probably too busy looking at the rest of her to notice, but I'm pretty sure they were blue.

My blood dripped down her wrinkly chin. She reached up with her left pointer finger, wiped the blood from her chin then put the blood-coated finger in her mouth and sucked it. She slowly wrapped her lips around the tip and then sucked my blood from her finger, all the way down to her hand. My hard-on was getting stiffer every second I watched this monster suck her finger. I wished I was that finger.

What am I seeing? Why the heck am I turned on? And what the hell is wrong with her face? Rick, get it together! Just focus on getting to work.

I was feeling pretty confused, so I picked up the pace to head straight to work. I worried I was delusional, or possibly still drunk from the night before. Maybe I needed more caffeine? I hoped the coffee would shake me of these visions — it felt like the last line of defense between me and a mental institution.

I finally arrived at work — late — and I just knew it was going to be a god-awful day. Just like every other day.

I was a Junior Sales Representative at Lightning Pop, home of Carlos' Coke. As impressive as that might sound, realistically it meant that I spent all day telling three people who to call to hawk soda. Sure, sometimes I got to make a phone call or two myself when shit got crazy, but that was only in a major crisis. Eighteen-wheelers full of soda weren't getting robbed or flipping over all that often, so the fact was, my job was utterly numbing. There was no authority or power in my position, and everyone who worked there had an insultingly low salary. That is, everyone but the entitled woman who had just barged through the front door of my office.

My boss. Hurricane Laura. She was a cold-hearted bitch with long, shiny black hair. She was a big-boned, thick woman — thick in a good way, a sexy way. She had all the right curves in all the right places. Her eyes were jet black and extremely bold — almost intimidating. Nothing got past those eyes. She wasn't nearly as attractive as the woman I'd been craving since the cafe that morning, but she was something for me to look at while I was at work.

Laura didn't knock when she forced the front door of my

office open and headed straight for me.

Shit, here we go.

"Good morning, Rick," she said, slamming her bags on my desk in front of me, covering up my work for the day.

Lady, please just do me a favor and fuck off. I never had the guts to be rude to her, even when she obviously deserved it.

"Hey, Laura." I nodded slightly, trying to ignore her. She walked to stand next to my chair and angled herself as she leaned over my desk so her cleavage was the only thing I could see. It was no accident that the top two buttons on her blouse were undone, and I could clearly see her black lace bra. She was doing her best to entice me in her not-so-subtle way.

"Looking good, Rick," she said. "Spending some extra time at the gym, are we? Your quads are looking thick," she purred as I tried to do something other than simply stare down her shirt, which was hard.

I was uncomfortable with her advancements, but I'd gotten used to it as part of the job, which was pretty messed up. *God, she's so inappropriate. Leave me alone, lady. Though if I have sex with her maybe she'll finally let me work in peace?* She came on to me so regularly that I'd inevitably thought about it before — more than once — but I wasn't interested in her. For one thing, she was my boss, and you don't shit where you eat.

"Nope. No gym for me." I gave a weak chuckle that I hoped would register as more pathetic than playful, but she continued to lean over me and flutter her eyelashes. *Damn, she really can't take a hint. I think somebody has some sexual harassment classes in her future.*

"I'm not much of a gym rat, Laura. If you don't mind, I

have a lot of work to do." Laura cracked a small smile knowing full well I didn't have a damn thing that had to be done at that moment. She moved to the other side of my desk and leaned forward so her tits were inches from my face.

Give it up already. Jesus Christ.

"I know your boss, Rick. Maybe you should try to play nice with her. It might even get you a promotion, or a raise. You could get very lucky." I sat still as a stone as she dangled her words in front of me alongside her breasts. I didn't flinch. She shook her shoulders a little so her chest jiggled. I sat still, my eyes glued to hers.

When she saw I was unmoved she frowned, stood up and crossed her arms with an audible 'Humph'.

Finally.

"Relax, Rick. I'm just trying to get a rise out of you…" She drew the words out and scanned me up and down. "I just wanted to stop by your desk, and see if you needed anything before I start my day."

Bullshit. You stopped by to harass me, as usual.

"Well, since you're here, I wanted to ask you about the Davis account," I said as I reached for one of the many folders on my desk.

"Do whatever you think is right, I trust you, Rick." She grabbed her bags and breezed out of my office as freely as she'd entered. Before shutting her own office door behind her she called out from across the hall, "Just don't screw me over," then made a big show of winking. I received dirty looks from the few other employees like clockwork. Laura smiled then closed the door firmly behind her.

She was a full-blown tease, and a terrible boss. I was not interested in her but my body parts had their own agenda: I was left in my office with a full-blown erection. Again.

How am I supposed to get any work done with this damn thing?

The growing bulge in my pants wasn't the first I'd experienced in the office. It was only half past nine a.m., which wasn't even the earliest Laura had dangled some of her parts in front of me, but my day had just started and work needed to get done. After all, nobody else was going to sell that soda for me. So it was either knuckle down and do the job, or wander into the bathroom to take care of myself while visualizing the goddess from Paul's Café. After spending a long time thinking I chose the soda…

Chapter Two

Lizzie watched the condensation bead into drops and slowly run down her glass of chilled wine. Her preferred brand was cheap and sweet like candy, with a mild hint of strawberry. She favored fresh blood directly from the vein — warm and thick — but in a pinch the pink wine would just about satisfy her cravings.

As she watched the droplets slide down the glass, she was reminded of the mind-blowing orgasms she used to have. Sweat beaded on her skin and trickled down her chest, running over her breasts and both of her nipples. The drips flowed downwards on her perfectly smooth stomach, eventually settling in the button of her belly. The sweat and her memories mingled as she gasped, and climaxed. She was unable to function for hours. Just the memory of having a huge cock firmly thrust deep inside her, over and over again, left her quaking and quivering.

She sat with her legs crossed on a black leather couch in the basement lounge of her hotel, composing herself while patiently waiting for her next meal. The leather was as soft and silky as her skin, and she loved the feel of it beneath her. Who would be her next victim? The solitary old man at the end of the bar, drowning his sorrows in cheap bourbon? No, too easy a target. Or perhaps the two men locked in embrace, rubbing each other on the couch directly across the lounge? One was wearing a blonde wig and hot pink lipstick while the other amorously rubbed the bewigged man's shoulders before leaning in for a kiss. Those two were not her taste, really. She thought the old man would probably have more fight in him than the gay lovers combined, and a cruel smirk crept to her lips. Lizzie enjoyed it when her victims were attracted to her so she could play, taunt, and enrage them; it made the hunt more exciting, and the kill infinitely more satisfying.

She turned her gaze to the tables in front of the lounge's empty stage and spotted him. Her next meal. She could feel hunger grow in her stomach just looking at him. He was unmistakably a businessman, likely on a business trip. He was probably married, and probably looking to cheat on his wife, though Lizzie hadn't spotted a wedding ring on his finger, so there was no way she could be sure of his situation. In any case, she was hungry, and he was there — a bad break for someone in the wrong place at the wrong time.

She fully intended to sit on his face to get off a few times before offing him, but her luck had run dry of late. Chances were, he was only going to be good for one thing that night, and she was willing to bet it wasn't going to be sex. The odds were good that he didn't know how to properly take care of a woman. Let alone one with her tastes. Ultimately her main objective was to drink him dry. She was choosy enough to reject the gay lovers, but it had been six days since her last kill; she was weak and yearning for fresh blood. She needed to eat, and couldn't afford to be too selective.

Lizzie got up from the couch and walked towards the man she was about to make her dinner. She passed the two men on the other couch and thought they were laying it on a bit thick. "Get a room," she groaned. They looked at her for a second before quickly returning their attention to each other.

She approached the man from behind, slowly, with an intent stare. She stalked her prey. That was always Lizzie's favorite part. She enjoyed the climax of the kill, of course, but taking the time to observe her victim was a kind of dark art. And Lizzie was one hell of an artist.

Once she reached the very unlucky man, she placed her right hand around the back of his neck. Carefully, she dug her nails into his skin with more than enough pressure to grab his attention. He turned to face her and slammed his empty glass down on the bar before him. The glass shattered and his thumb caught a jagged edge. Blood ran out of his digit and down into his hand. He looked at Lizzie and his expression was completely blank. He was extremely drunk.

She saw and smelled the blood from his hand and her eyes began to glow red, radiating out from the center of her pupils, which she could feel dilating. She hoped the drunk wouldn't make a scene over her changing eyes, blowing her cover. But his eyes were glazed and unfocused as he stared at her through his stupor.

She whispered in his ear, "Come with me — I promise it'll be worth it." She ran her tongue along his ear and tasted the salt on his sweating skin. She gently bit the base of his earlobe. Lizzie grabbed his tie firmly and pulled him off his stool. He fell to the floor and landed hard. She knew if he hadn't been drinking, he would have been in serious pain, and would have been seriously troublesome. Lizzie pulled him back to his feet, and dragged him out of the lounge. He didn't fight her... Not that he could have, even if he'd wanted to.

She half-carried him out of the lounge and they stepped onto the carpeted red floors of the hotel lobby. This felt like kismet, given that in just a few minutes the man's body was going to match the color of the carpet perfectly. Lizzie yanked him towards the elevator. She was always careful to notice and then avoid security cameras, but luckily there weren't any in this particular lobby.

The drunk fool was practically unable to walk on his own. His head lolled against her breasts and his hand slipped down behind her and groped for her ass. Even blind drunk, he was a typical man — Lizzie rolled her glowing red eyes in annoyance. She hated being thought of as the prey.

"Wait until we get to the room. I promise we'll get to the fun part soon, baby." She pushed the up button and the cold steel doors of the elevator yawned open. She was happy to find the elevator empty, though she had an immediate urge to kill him.

Lizzie could have ripped his throat out with her bare hands and nobody would have ever known that she was there or what she did to him. Someone would have found his dead body lifelessly riding a bloody elevator, but that wouldn't have any effect on her; she would be long gone before that ever happened. She would have thoroughly enjoyed killing him in the elevator — their elevator — but opted against leaving a bloody mess. After all, she had a giant hotel room that she needed to use for something. What was she going to do? Sleep?! She chuckled to herself: Lizzie never slept.

They reached the 19th floor and she dragged him out of the elevator with one hand. She dragged him behind her all the way down the hall, and to the door of her room. The man had already passed out. Lizzie's suspicions were yet again confirmed; all men were pathetic. And nearly all of them were only good for one thing: feeding.

Lizzie pulled her key card from the inside of her bra, swiped it through the handle and unlocked the hotel room. As she did, the drunkard fell sideways against the wall and slid down to the floor. She picked him up yet again, and flicked the light switch upon entering the room.

The room was open and spacious. There was a large bed on the left, and a recliner sat in front of the picture window, which ran the whole length of the back wall. A large bathroom was in the corner of the suite with a tidy toilet, a sink, and a shower that could fit ten people.

"What's going on?" he slurred. He looked up at her in his stupor but managed to ask her, "Where am I?"

"Don't you remember me, baby? You met me downstairs and said that you were looking for a good time." She shoved him firmly away and he bounced onto the bed and on his back.

"Wow, you're really strong…" he slurred again. He looked puzzled, but that didn't stop him from trying to shrug off his suit coat while loosening his tie. He was very confused, but even that didn't stop him from hoping he was about to get lucky.

"You have no idea." She tore his tie from his neck with her sharp claws, instantly shredding it to tiny pieces that fluttered around him on the bed.

"How the heck did you rip my tie like that?" he asked woozily. He was oblivious to what she was going to do to him. He lowered the straps of her dress to expose her bra and abdomen, and then dropped her dress to the floor. He was blind drunk, but could see well enough to be stunned by Lizzie's beauty.

"Oh, I have many talents, baby. Like what you see?" She was almost naked.

Lizzie reached down as if to coax down the zipper of his pants, but then tore his pants completely off so he lay before her in just his boxers and socks. She climbed on top of him in nothing but her bra and panties. She kissed his neck and chest, pressing her body against his. She could feel his cock stiffening as she grinded up against him. She pulled off her bra leaving him to do whatever he wanted with her breasts. She moaned as he pinched one and tried to suck on the other, but was too drunk to sit up enough to get them in his mouth. He gave up trying and simply laid back, attempting to seductively blow on her tits. He wheezed and sputtered.

Lizzie worked her way down his body, sucking and kissing, licking and biting. She slid off his boxers. When she fell to her knees, she was faced with his semi-impressive erection, so she started kissing the sides of his cock below the head and eventually put the tip of it in her mouth.

"Holy shit. My wife doesn't do that any more. Keep going. Don't stop," the man said as he begged her to continue.

Lizzie had her lips wrapped around him as she slid her mouth up and down his shaft. He clutched the satin sheets of the bed tight in his fists, and she put all of him into her throat. She wanted to get it over with so she could get to the fun part — eating. She was starved. "I'm going to blow. Keep doing that. Don't stop." She wished he would just come already.

As she gobbled him up one last time, he released his whole load in the back of her throat and she swallowed every last drop. She knew she was good, but even she was surprised at how quickly he had just cum.

"How was that for you? Do you feel better now?" she asked while rubbing his thighs. She turned her head so he wouldn't see that her front fangs were starting to grow, which happened whenever she was hungry and horny.

"I haven't had a blow job from my wife in years. You were amazing. We should do this again sometime... I really should be getting back to my room now. I need to sleep this off before morning. I have an early meeting tomorrow."

Lizzie wondered if the man noticed her fangs. She got up off her knees in just her thong and when he tried to get up, she pushed him back onto the bed again with force.

"Sorry, baby, but you're not going anywhere. Now it's my turn." She slowly crawled up on top of him and pinned down both his arms She opened her mouth wide. The man could now clearly see the razor-sharp fangs in her mouth. The look of fear bled into his eyes.

"What are you doing? Why can't I move?" he asked her, terrified. "And what the hell is wrong with your teeth? They're... huge." The fear he was starting to feel snowballed and showed itself in his wavering voice.

"That's the point, you're not going to move." She paused. "It will be over quick though, I promise. And as for my teeth? I have terrific oral hygiene." She laughed at her own joke. He was trying to fight her off of him, but it was useless; she had him trapped.

"What're you going to do? Please! You can't kill me..." the man pleaded with her.

"I absolutely can kill you. I kill bad men like you all the time. You're one of the lucky ones, though, most guys don't get an incredible blow job before they die. So for that, you're welcome." Lizzie rested her hand on top of his head.

In one seamless motion she shoved his head into a pillow to expose his neck, and sank her teeth into his exposed flesh. He screamed and gurgled as she pushed her fangs further and further into his jugular. His screams were getting louder, so she covered his mouth with her other hand. He kicked his legs and thrashed wildly on the bed. He tried repeatedly to push her off, but she was too strong. He was a helpless victim, and she was in complete control.

Lizzie could feel the man's blood rush straight to her head. She loved the feeling that human blood gave her. It made her feel stronger and faster in every way. It made her feel euphoric. Her favorite high was induced by human blood; it fed her and it healed her. She could mend and repair herself with time — perks of being a vampire — but human blood always got her there quicker.

The man's legs stopped frantically kicking and she could feel his pulse start to weaken in her mouth. She savored each drop of blood, enjoying it just as much as the pathetic man had enjoyed cumming in her mouth. She was having a wonderful time killing him. Eventually his heartbeat stopped completely, and there was no more screaming or fight left in him. There was no heartbeat, no struggle, and nothing left for her to drink.

Lizzie had drained the nameless man utterly dry, leaving him a desiccated corpse. She licked her lips and was satisfied for the time being. She had just finished eating, and needed to clean herself up.

Lizzie stood on the tan and white marble floor in the bathroom of the hotel room she had rented the night before. She stared at herself in the mirror as she always did after a good night of feeding. Even though it was only her own kind that could see her reflection, she loved looking at her own beauty. Wearing only her bra and panties, she reached for the faucet to let the water run hot. Steam started to fill the room as she looked at her reflection. She noticed a small trace of cum dripping from the inside of her left thigh down her leg. Lizzie wasn't sure how it got there, given the john had come in her mouth, but he could have cum again when he was dying — she had been too busy drinking him dry to notice or care.

The grey washcloth she used to clean herself was resting on the right side of the sink. She grabbed it and began to ring it out. As she squeezed it, blood dripped from the washcloth down the sides of the sink and into the drain. She wiped off her thigh and looked back into the mirror. A few drops of blood had run down the left side of her mouth and dried alongside her smeared lipstick.

"Missed a spot. Can't leave looking like I just ate some jerk." She laughed out loud as she grabbed a paper towel from above the porcelain sink.

She walked back into the bedroom, switching off the bathroom light as she did. She had almost forgotten about the messy corpse, lying in a pool of blood which had soaked the sheets. He was on his back, cold and naked. His arms were above his head, and his neck was covered in blood and bite marks. She leaned in to give him a kiss on his blue lips. His empty eyes stared back at her.

It had been so easy for her to seduce this piece of shit and get exactly what she had wanted it was almost embarrassing. She picked up his belt, which was draped over the end of the bed, and suddenly cracked him with it across his chest. She reveled in the loud noise made by the leather smacking against his flesh. Her midnight snack had been too drunk to have any fun after the blow job. If this corpse was still able to experience regret, he would have felt it acutely after she started whipping. She hit him again, and again. Over and over until she felt relief, adding more welts and marks to the already damaged and beaten corpse. Then she put the belt down and leaned over the body to spit on his chest. She was going to continue to humiliate him and reduce him to nothing, even in death. To her, he was just another scumbag — a pile of dirt beneath her feet. Somebody who'd wanted her for one thing, and one thing only. Sex. Meaningless and horrible sex, which he didn't even get. He was just like every other man.

She had meant nothing to him, so she killed him. Simple as that. She was also hungry, so she'd popped open his jugular with her front fangs and drank every last drop of his blood. While she drank him, she had seen every recent memory and fleeting thought in this idiot's brain. She saw him fucking hooker after hooker. Then she saw his wife and children thinking daddy was their hero, even after he beat them for no reason other than he'd wanted to. Lizzie had known a lot of pieces of shit, and this idiot — like all other pieces of shit — deserved everything Lizzie had just given him.

His blood was like the sweet wine from the previous night but without the strawberry taste; steaming hot, and much more metallic. Lizzie enjoyed tasting him and dominating him, and drinking him in while showing him that she was in control. A superior genus, stronger and faster than any human. She was a creature of the night. She was a vampire.

The pathetic bastard thought he was going to get a night of amazing sex with a beautiful woman then leave her. Lizzie had seen his thoughts. And, while he certainly got some pleasure that night, Lizzie had gotten more. She had gotten off while sucking his life from his veins. He had come once, quickly, died, then came again. Pathetic.

Hours passed and Lizzie searched her home — the

contents of a Samsonite 421 XL suitcase — for something to wear. That same suitcase had been her home for the last twenty years while she searched for a place to settle. Though she'd been in New York City for a while, she still didn't technically have a place of her own. A place to call her home.

Lizzie was still in her bra and panties, which always matched and typically complemented her beautiful, blonde hair. She loved to be in her undergarments — she had no qualms showing off and sharing her assets, but her tits and ass had no problem gaining attention in or out of her clothes. If her figure didn't get the attention she desired (which almost never happened), her tattoos almost always certainly did. There were hummingbirds of all colors flitting along her left rib cage, surrounded by black roses that curled around her stomach, ending in her pierced belly button. The artwork was extremely intricate and detailed, and was exquisitely displayed on her forever-young, toned body. She was flawless.

Even though she was gorgeous to look at, which she knew, Lizzie wasn't always happy with herself. She wasn't the woman she once was. Sometimes she was consumed with hatred for what she had become. She had loved before, and she had been loved. Things used to be different. Things used to be simpler. But that was when she had been human. That was before she ripped out throats for fun.

Chapter Three

I shuffled some papers around my desk as I stared at the clock, willing the incessant workday to finally end. The ticking second hand used to bring me comfort during my utterly predictable workdays, but now it taunted me with every click, click, click — like the telltale heart of a less-boring life.

God. Won't this day just end, already? I need a drink. It was all I could think about. Drinking was the most exciting thing in my life, and I'd decided to just lean in. Why not? Once I was freed from the workday I could go home and do nothing. And drink. Just like every other goddamn day.

I needed a drink. Though, I wouldn't have minded having the girl from the café this morning. I would take her over the alcohol any day. She would definitely be more entertaining than a bottle of gin, and I'm sure she could take the edge off. Damn... she was something else.

I grabbed the folder at the bottom of the pile of work I was avoiding to check the schedule for the rest of the week. I rubbed my eyeballs because the schedule looked like a fuzzy, ink-riddled mess, but then realized it was because every day was full of appointments, and the rest of the week was booked solid. I would be having some more very long days.

Looks like Thursday is going to be a long one. Especially with the new Davis account. Ugh. No, thank you. Maybe if I'm nice to Laura... that bitch will...

I knew cozying up to my temperamental boss probably wouldn't make any difference, but I really didn't want to work. I tossed the manila folder back on the pile, shut my eyes tight and wished for the work to magically disappear — dispatched by some magical fairy godmother, but the pile was still there when I opened my eyes; I was the only fairy godmother who had to tackle the mindless work. With a sigh, I got up to head to Laura's office when I had a sudden urge to run to the bathroom. Immediately. *Time for a quick detour, I guess. Anything to put off kissing Laura's ass.*

I rushed past the cubicles and down the hall to the bathroom, compelled by how horribly I suddenly needed to go.

Shit, that came on quick. I didn't even drink that much today. To Hell with middle age.

I eagerly leaned my body against the swinging bathroom door, ready for relief. Instead of opening, though, the door barely budged. There was a great amount of resistance, like someone pushing with their full weight to keep the door shut from inside the bathroom. I shoved myself against it with a grunt, and, with my shoulder pressed to the aluminum door, a man on the other side quickly pulled it open to yank me inside.

He was wearing a hood that completely covered his head except for a small hole in the front, where I could just barely make out his face.

"We need to talk, Rick," he said as he pulled the hood off his head.

I recognized that deep quiet voice, and I knew that terrifying face under the shiny bald pate. It was all too familiar. Towering over me in the Lightning Pop employee bathroom was Christo's right-hand man, his number two, Lazarus Bedding.

"Lazarus?!" I choked out. "What the hell are you doing here? Shouldn't you be at the dry cleaners? Or off catering to your douchebag boss?" The towering lackey looked almost frightened as he stood silently in the center of the grimy bathroom. I'd never known this three-hundred-pound behemoth to be afraid of anything, except maybe Christo.

I caught my reflection in the mirror above the sink, and my reflection looked as worried as Lazarus did standing before me. His reflection was, well, missing; mirror-me was alone in the bathroom.

What the hell?

Puzzled and confused, I turned back to Lazarus.

"Listen Rick, there's no time to tell you everything. I can't explain things to you right now. Just know that you need to be extremely careful. There's a lot of bad shit happening that you couldn't even begin to understand. You will, in time, but if I tried to explain right now, you'd try to lock me in a padded room and throw away the key."

He's right. He sounds totally, batshit crazy. Lazarus being on edge, though — that's a new one. I wonder what's got him so upset?

"C'mon, man. What the fuck are you talking about? You're way out of line, and starting to kind of scare me. You should try to calm down, Lazarus —you look like you've seen a ghost."

He was jittery and sweating. Rather than explain to me why he'd strong-armed me into that smelly room, he tried to push through me to leave, but I blocked the door. He could have easily overpowered me, but he was so nervous that his strength seemed to leave him. And I wasn't about to let him go without some explanation.

"Rick, I need to go." He put his massive hand on my shoulder in a not-entirely-friendly way. "Now. Just know — I didn't have a choice, and I'm really sorry you've gotten mixed up in all of this."

Uh-oh, what's he talking about? Mixed up in what exactly?

"I don't know how much they'll tell you right now, but you might be able to get some answers from Maryanne or Paul." His heavy hand was feeling heavier by the second, but he still hadn't really told me anything.

"What? Answers to what? How am I supposed to get answers when I don't even know what the *questions* are?" He was clearly unimpressed with my frustration because, instead of giving me more information, Lazarus shoved me away from the door with a guttural grunt.

OW. Damn, man. Did he just growl at me? He traps me in a bathroom cage and then growls at me like a damn animal... Just my luck.

He hurriedly pushed past me and left. Before I could turn around to grab him, he was gone.

Okay... that was a lot... And I still need to piss.

After I relieved myself, I splashed some cold water on my face from the cracked sink to make sure I wasn't in a dream. The droplets hit the mirror, my face, and my poor excuse for a work shirt, leaving an unsightly wet spot. As unfortunate as it was, this was my reality and I wasn't dreaming.

Okay, go to the café right after work to talk to Paul and Maryanne. They'll be helpful, right? Man up, Rick!

I left the bathroom where Lazarus and I had just had our tete-a-tete to get the conversation with Laura out of the way. All I could think about was getting to the cafe, but my boss would skin me alive if I didn't clear my schedule with her first. Dreading the conversation that was about to take place, I walked slowly and prayed it would take until tomorrow to reach her office. Sadly, it did not.

This is all I need... just the icing on the cake of an already shitty day. Oh, how I love dealing with this insane woman.

I reached Laura's office and noticed that the blinds on her door window were all the way down and louvered so I couldn't see in, which was pretty unusual. She was an exhibitionist, if nothing else. I tapped on the door. I knocked twice and waited for an answer. Nothing. I knocked again two more times, harder than before. Still, no reply.

That's odd. *She never ignores me.*

I turned around to scan the cubicles and found just one person left in the office, so I hollered over to him. Tony in accounting — a genuinely nice guy, but a little nerdier than me, if possible.

"Hey, Tony! Is Laura in her office right now?" I barked across the room, trying to make it clear I wasn't interested in conversation.

"Yep. Last I knew she'd been in there all afternoon." Tony replied casually. "How are things going with you, Rick?"

"That's what I thought — I'm just gonna go in. Maybe she's on the phone, or something. Thanks, Tony."

Good job, Rick. Another pleasant conversation successfully avoided.

Tony smiled. I gave him a small wave and returned my attention to Laura's office. *I wonder if her door is locked... Dummy, you didn't even check the knob.*

I grabbed the doorknob and turned it. Sure enough, it was unlocked. The door swung open, and I saw the top of Laura's head peeking from behind her oversized faux-leather chair. She was seated facing the large bay window, her back to me. Tresses of her long hair hung over the back of the chair, knotted.

"Hey, Laura. I was wondering if we could maybe change the schedule for Thursday afternoon? It looks like it's going to be a late night, and we had to stay late two nights last week, so…" I was hoping for a little sympathy, but she didn't respond. *The silent treatment? Seriously?*

"Laura? What do you think about Thursday? I've already made plans with friends for after work that night."

She knows I don't have any friends. I'm obviously trying here, though throw me a bone, lady!

Still no answer from the boss lady.

Come ON. What the fuck?

I walked up to her chair and placed my hand near her hair, which was sure to get a reaction. Instead, again, I got nothing. I could feel something sticky on the pads of my fingers. Bringing my hand into the light from the bay window, I saw my fingers had been stained red.

What the hell? Is that blood?

Her office was quiet. Slowly, I turned Laura's chair around. She was propped up, dead in her chair. Her throat had been slit, and her neck and chest were slick with her own blood. The tan carpet under her chair had gone crimson, soaked with her blood. Laura's eyes were wide open and it felt like she was looking right at me.

"Oh, my God! Tony, call 911!" I yelled from where I stood.

"What? Rick, is everything okay?" Tony yelled back.

"No! Everything is not okay! Just dial the phone, Tony!"

"I'm on it! What should I say to them?"

I was still staring at Laura as Tony and I shouted across the small office. "Tell them there's been a murder, and that they need to get here right away." Yelling the words made it real.

"Oh, my God. A murder?" I could hear Tony finally make the call. "Yes, hello? 911? My name is Tony Pratt and I'm an accountant at Lightning Pop and we need an ambulance and the police right away... Someone was murdered in the office...! I don't know, just send everybody."

He slammed the phone back on its base before running to join me in Laura's office.

Tony made it to the door of Laura's office and stopped in his tracks. Seated before him, and staring straight ahead, was the blood-stained body of the woman who used to be his boss. He was still for half a second before he fiercely grabbed my arm, and let out a high-pitched scream.

"Holy shit... Laura... she's dead. She's dead!"

"Yeah, I can see that, Tony." I pried his fingers off my arm and shoved him aside. "What did they say on the phone?"

Tony just stood there, in shock.

"Tony!" I yelled at the top of my lungs. "Snap out of it. What did they say on the phone?"

Tony began to spit out parts of a sentence. "Police. Ambulance. On the way..."

With my luck this moron was probably gonna think I killed her.

"Rick... did you do this to her?" Tony asked.

Fucking predictable. What an idiot.

"No, Tony. I didn't do this. Why would you even ask that?"

In all fairness he wasn't totally off-base to ask the guy who found her, I guess. The EMTs arrived a few minutes later, followed immediately by the police. The first EMT in the room looked like he'd just graduated high school — a tall and blonde kid with a baby face. He walked in the office and pointed directly at Laura with an accusatory index finger.

"I'm guessing this is why you called us? So, which one of you did it?" he asked Tony and me while smiling. His attempt to lighten the mood did not work. *Great. A funny guy. That was all this situation needed.*

"We didn't do this," Tony snapped. "Well, I didn't anyways."

Thank you, Tony, for throwing me under the bus.

"My name is Rick Blume, and I didn't do this either. Honestly. I am the one who found her, though." I didn't want to incriminate myself, but I also realized in that moment, I didn't really know how to not look suspicious. A short, fat detective appeared from behind the EMT and immediately filled the room. Between me, Tony, the farm boy EMT, Laura's corpse and the detective's gut, the room was getting cramped.

"I'm Detective Jackson Lee." He tipped his hat. "Can you tell me what happened, son?" he asked me in a deep tone.

Son? I'm pretty sure I'm thirty-six, Detective.

"I'm a sales representative here. Laura is my... well, she was my boss."

"All right, then." He scribbled something in a tattered notebook. It was like his entire detective persona was based on detectives he'd seen in movies and on TV. "Tell me, fella, did you spend any special time with her outside of work?" he asked as he looked around her office.

No. I wasn't sleeping with my boss, especially after her

constant sexual harassment. I thought better of mentioning this but could feel my palms starting to sweat.

"No sir, I never saw her outside of work."

Just stay calm, Rick. You didn't do this. Keep breathing. I wasn't sure why I was trying to convince myself.

The fat man hiked up his trousers with one hand. "And what about you?" he asked, turning to Tony. "Did she have any enemies that you know of?"

Laura? Enemies? Umm, I'm pretty sure that was all she had.

Tony took a minute before he answered. "Not that I can think of. Everyone loved Laura. She was a great lady and a fantastic boss. We couldn't have asked for a better person here around the office." Tony looked almost weepy.

Great lady? Are we talking about the corpse? Come on, Tony. She was horrible at making friends, and worse at keeping them.

The fat detective didn't look convinced. "And neither of you two helpful gentlemen saw anything suspicious here today?" he asked, narrowing his pudgy eyes to slits.

Lazarus was here today. Moments ago, actually. But do I mention it? I had almost completely forgotten about the strange encounter in the bathroom amidst the chaos.

"So nobody noticed anything odd today?" he asked again.

"I had just finished up in the bathroom when I came in to ask her about a scheduling change for Thursday. This is how I found her. Look, I still have blood on my fingers from touching the chair" I raised my hand to show that I wasn't lying.

Way to make yourself look guilty, Rick... Literally red-handed.

Detective Lee grabbed my hand and pulled it closer to

him.

"Why do you have blood on your fingers?" he asked sternly. "Did you touch the victim in any way?"

I knew that I was now being considered a suspect.

"I set my hand at the top of her chair to get her attention. When I picked up my hand, I saw the blood and turned her chair around. She was dead and... Just dead!"

Detective Lee released my hand.

"So you say. All right, well, that's an interesting story but I think that'll be it for the moment. I'll get the coroner in here to get her body out of here, at some point. Neither of you leave the city, y'hear me? Not until I get all of this straightened out. I'll also get in touch with the security company to get the footage from today. I assure you I will get to the bottom of this; we'll get the bastard who did this," he proclaimed to the room.

"That will be great, Detective," I answered helpfully. "Thank you." I never left the city anyways, so no problem there.

They don't have anything on you, so take a breath, Rick. There were security cameras all over this place so he'd probably see Lazarus somewhere on those tapes... I probably should have told him, but he was accusing me so fuck him.

The fat detective left Lightning Pop, leaving the medical examiners to do their jobs. Tony was standing outside of Laura's office, white as a ghost. I was experiencing a whirlwind of emotions, naturally, but Tony looked like he was on the brink of a total breakdown.

Should I say something? I should say something.

"Are you all right?" I asked, hoping Tony would ignore me the way I always tried to ignore him.

"Rick, that was my first time seeing a dead body. I'm

feeling kind of shaken, I guess. I'm sorry," Tony offered earnestly.

"No reason for an apology. It was my first dead body, too. Try not to worry; we'll get to the bottom of this. One way or another," I said, trying to calm him.

"This is too much for one day, I think," said Tony. "I just want to go home, if that's all right."

"Yeah, go ahead. Try to get some rest. We can touch base tomorrow."

Tony has been a constant annoyance for years. But right now, I actually feel really bad for him.

Tony left quickly. I could hear his sniffling nose run all the way to the parking lot. He was shaken, but we had just found the still-bleeding corpse of someone we knew. In the office. With her throat cut. Laura had been a bitch, for sure. But she didn't deserve to be murdered. Not like that.

Well, this has been a red-letter day... I can taste the gin already...

I gathered my things. The medical examiners would be a while and there was nothing more for me to do. I had already managed to make myself a suspect in the two minutes of questioning with the detective. It was time for me to go.

The walk back through the city seemed much more tedious than usual. Walking was not a chore because, typically, I was interested in and aware of my surroundings — curious what the tall, leggy brunette did to deserve three police officers' attention — or if there were still people trapped in the burning apartment building surrounded by six fire trucks. But not today.

I was halfway through an intersection when I saw the light at the crosswalk telling me to stop.

Shit. Shit. Shit!

A yellow taxi was barreling down on me, its horn blaring, telling me to get the fuck out of the street. I saw it come toward me as if in slow-motion until I dove at the last second, the tires skidding on the pavement and the cabbie's epithets streaming from the open windows. I landed in a heap on the edge of the sidewalk as the taxi flew by me. I got up to brush myself off, still thinking of the gin I was going to gulp shortly and I could tell I had scraped my knee. It stung, but I was in one piece so I didn't investigate too much. I was shaken up, bruised, and thirsty. It had been one hell of a day and I was lucky to be alive.

Chapter Four

I arrived at the café with no idea of what was going to happen next. I was disoriented and shaken from almost being killed by the taxi, and my knee hurt like hell.

Shit... I wonder if it's broken. That would've been all I needed.

I felt shooting pains rip through my knee with every step so I grabbed the stool closest to the door, rather than my usual table, as all I could focus on was taking pressure off of my mangled leg. I sat at the counter, wincing, and waited to be attended to. Maryanne noticed me from across the café. She smiled casually as she walked towards me with her face buried in her cell phone, but her expression quickly changed when she saw that something about me was off. She set her phone on the counter next to me.

I hope she doesn't ask me about my day. Where would I even start?

I knew I looked even rougher than usual, and that she could tell that I was in pain. I remembered Lazarus telling me to get answers from Paul and Maryanne, but I had no idea what to ask them. Or why.

"Hey, Rick. Long time," Maryanne joked, before her expression turned serious. "You look like you've had a rough day," she said while wiping the counter in front of me with a wet cloth.

Yup. Here we go.

"Yeah, well, it's been a really weird day. Plus, I was almost hit by a taxi on the way here." I poured some sugar into the black coffee Maryanne had brought to me unprompted. She was always so nice to me, and I'd always wondered why. Looking back, it's easy to see the people who were only nice when they needed something, but not Maryanne. She was one of the nicest and most caring people I knew.

"Oh, my goodness! Rick, are you all right? Should I call a doctor? I could take you to the hospital. Lemme just let Paul know, real quick."

That is NOT happening. I am not going to have you drag me to a hospital just to wait for six hours before even being seen.

"No, no. I'm fine. Just scraped my knee a little. It's no big deal, and I'm sure it'll be fine in a day or two." I hoped I sounded convincing — I really, really hated the hospital — but my knee also really hurt. A lot.

She knows I'm lying. I'm a terrible liar.

"Are you sure, because you look like you should probably see a doctor, or something," she persisted. "Honestly, you're looking pretty rough."

Let's talk about my day, shall we? It's gone from finding my boss with her throat slit in her office, to almost getting killed by some idiot taxi driver on my way here. And now my knee is fucking killing me. So, yeah. It's been a very shitty day.

"Really, Maryanne. I truly appreciate your concern, and sincere thanks for the compliment on how great I look today, but I promise you — I'll be fine." I knew this wouldn't put her off the scent; I was probably the worst liar I ever met, and I knew I looked worse than I normally did.

"You have a car, don't you? Is there some reason you didn't drive to work today?" She was always prying into my business, but maybe she legitimately cared about what happened to me, which I wasn't used to — somebody caring, that is.

"My engine shit the bed last week, and I can't afford to fix it at the moment."

When it rains it pours…

"I'm really sorry to hear that. If you ever need a ride, or anything, don't hesitate to ask. Whatever you need, I'm here for you." She placed her hand over mine on the counter and smiled at me. Her cheeks began to turn rosy red.

"Well, actually, something happened today that I was kind of hoping I could talk to you about. You and Paul. In private…" I leaned over the counter so she could hear me whisper, "I don't have any idea of what's going on. And I know I look like shit, but that's because I'm totally freaking out… I'm really scared."

She leaned to get closer to me and whispered in response, "There's no one else in here right now, Rick. It's just you and me. And Paul, of course. You can tell me anything, and I promise it will stay between us." My throbbing knee had completely distracted me from the fact the café was completely empty.

"Why don't you start by telling me what happened? Then we can get Paul if we need him." She held my hand even tighter, and I felt uncharacteristically comfortable talking to her; she was keeping me calm, and I felt safe trusting her. She was always kind to me, but I could tell that today she genuinely wanted to take care of me, protect me. Maryanne was always a great waitress, but today she was sending vibes that were more intimate than usual. It was disarming.

Well, here goes nothing. She's gonna think I'm nuts. Still, she asked.

"Well, for starters, Lazarus showed up at my job today." I took a sip of my coffee and wanted to spit it back into my cup because it was too hot. I felt it burn my throat as I gulped it down quickly instead. "I ran into him in the bathroom," I added sarcastically. I could tell by her expression that she was confused. She was gently rubbing the backs of my fingers with hers, which was both comforting, and unusual.

She's never held my hand like this before. Why the hell is everyone acting so strange today? Like, seriously — am I losing my mind?!

"Do you mean Lazarus as in big and tall, creepy, bald Lazarus? Christo's idiot sidekick?" she asked, smirking.

"Yes, Maryanne, *that* Lazarus. He's the only Lazarus *I* know of," I snapped sarcastically, thinking how horrible it would be to live in a world with more than one Lazarus.

"Yes, yes, good point. One is more than enough..." She stopped rubbing my hand and slowly backed away from the counter. "Okay, what happened after you saw him?"

What does she know about Lazarus that I don't?

"Maryanne, I can't make sense of what's going on right now — my life is a total shitshow. If there's anything you can tell me to, like, get a handle on things... I need help." I winced as my bum knee hit the underside of the counter. "And I haven't even told you the worst part yet." I shuddered: Laura's lifeless eyes staring at me over the rivers of her blood was an image seared into the front of my brain. Whenever I closed my eyes, her mangled corpse was the only thing I could see.

"So, tell me the worst of it, Rick. I'm here for you, you

know that." She placed her hand on mine again. Her hands were silky smooth.

"I know you are, and I really appreciate having someone to talk to. Really. Especially after the day from hell."

She leaned over the counter, like she wanted to be closer to me. The ends of her long brunette hair playfully brushed my hand. I had never wanted Maryanne in a sexual way until that moment. I was drawn to her, but not in the same way as the blonde from that morning. But Maryanne's comforting was undeniably turning me on.

"Tell me what happened, Rick," she pleaded. I stared at her as I weighed whether I should tell her about Laura, or not. With a deep sigh, I realized I had to tell her.

"It's my boss, Laura. She's dead. Fucking dead." My eyes began to tear up, which was a surprise since I'd absolutely hated Laura. "I found her. In her office. Her throat had been slit from ear to ear." Maryanne's face drained of all color.

"Rick, that's awful. I'm so sorry you're going through this." Maryanne squeezed my hand tightly, once, before her tone shifted. "Her throat was slit? Were there any other wounds on the body, that you could see?" Maryanne was looking at me with the most serious look I'd ever seen on her face. "Did you see any small punctures in her skin? Like, on her neck?"

Like, bite marks? From an animal? Why would she even ask that?

"Listen, Maryanne, I'm really not in the mood. I just told you her throat was slit. Her office was covered with her blood. I had gone to—"

"No, no, no, honey," she cut in, mid-sentence. "You don't understand. Let me go get Paul."

She backed away from the counter and headed for the

kitchen where I could see Paul attempting to mop the floor. He was splashing water all over the place. When she got to him, she grabbed his arm and stood on her tiptoes to whisper something in his ear. She had to crane her neck to his cupped ear as he towered over her by at least a foot. Whatever Maryanne whispered to him prompted him to drop his mop and look directly at me huddled and wincing at the counter.

What did she say to him?

They both emerged from the kitchen, looking straight at me. The seconds it took for them to reach my sad stool from the dirty kitchen door seemed like an hour, like watching my life in slow-motion. Step by step they came closer, and my heart beat faster and faster. I had no reason to fear them, but I did feel afraid.

These are two of the nicest people you've ever met, Rick. Take it easy. This is going to be fine. Everything is going to be just fine.

When Paul finally reached the counter he stood in front, the stained Formica between us. He was wearing his standard get-up: denim jeans with large holes at the knees, a light blue button up shirt with the top two buttons undone, and that damn sapphire necklace. He never took it off, and it always irked me.

Maryanne stood directly behind him, her eyes cast downward like a soldier waiting for her orders.

"Rick. Maryanne tells me you've had an eventful day," he said solemnly, never taking his eyes off of me.

"That's one way to put it," I scoffed. "I'd call it pretty fucked up, Paul." He was huge and I was scared, but my patience for all this secrecy and drama crap was wearing thin. "I mean, unless you consider finding your boss dead in her office 'eventful'. Then, yeah, my day was jam packed full of events!" I was shouting, but Paul cracked a small smile and stuffed his hands deep into his pockets.

"Sorry, Paul, I'm not trying to be a dick. It's just, today has been nuts."

"No worries, man. Take a breath; I think we can offer you some insight." He pulled a zippo from his pocket and flicked it open and shut a few times without lighting it.

Insight on what? I'd never been so confused. And I still had no idea what questions I should be asking.

"Maryanne. Lock it down." With this Maryanne deftly, dutifully locked the door and flipped the sign over to CLOSED. Nobody else would be coming in now. It was just them, and me.

Oh, great. He's going to kill me... Get yourself together, man.

I didn't actually think he was going to kill me, but the whole situation was making me very nervous, and I was on edge.

"Rick, follow me," he barked.

"Where are we going?" I asked worriedly.

"Get your ass off of that stool and follow me. Please," he again demanded, this time a little more politely.

I tried to rise from my stool and the counter in one fluid motion but my knee still hurt like hell. I winced my way to standing then waited for Paul to lead the way. He led Maryanne and me through the kitchen and into the back storage room. I'd expected everything to smell of dishwater and that mop Paul was always pushing aimlessly over the tiles, but it smelled like freshly-ground coffee, like how I imagined the whole country of Colombia smelling. On the back wall of the storage room was a very large freezer. Paul walked to the freezer and paused, giving me a solemn look.

What's he going to do? Beat me with some frozen chicken and stuff me inside? God, I hope not.

"Listen, Rick, I need you to promise me that you're never going to tell anybody about what you're about to see... I'm trusting you with my life's secrets here."

I blithely agreed, not fully appreciating the terms of this promise. "Sure, Paul. No problem. I'm a steel vault." An easy claim to make when I didn't know just what I'd be keeping secret.

He grabbed the freezer's handle with one hand and pushed a button hidden underneath with his other. There was a CLUNK, whiiiiiiiiiir. The whole freezer began to move. It rose from off the floor and then receded into the wall, revealing a dark stairway leading down. Paul, it seemed, had a hidden basement.

"Holy shit!" I exclaimed. "Are... are we going down there?" I really didn't want to go down a set of secret, spooky stairs — not after my hard day, not with a bum knee, not ever. But I sensed the stairs were not optional.

Paul grabbed my shoulder and gave me a gentle nudge towards the stairway that seemed to lead to a pit of darkness. I had never been a huge fan of the dark, but this was something far scarier.

"Let's go, Rick. Boy, do you have a lot to learn," Paul said as he pushed me into the void.

The stairwell was bitter cold and cloaked in shadow. The only illumination was from small white LED lights evenly placed along each side of the wall. We reached the bottom of the stairs and stepped onto a large emerald green carpet. I'm not sure what I was expecting, but this wasn't it. The carpet was spongy under the soles of my shoes and stained with brown and red splotches.

Is that blood? I had seen enough blood for one day.

Parts of the carpet had been torn and frayed by something very sharp. Almost like it had been mauled by a bear, or something bigger.

There was a yellow and green couch on the right side of the room that looked like it had seen considerably more action than I had. There were deep gouges and claw marks across the back, and one of the cushions' covers lay pitifully tattered.

I feel you, couch. Looks like you've known better days. But I guess, so have I.

I wasn't convinced that I actually had seen better days, but the couch didn't need to know that. The back wall was padded with a large white and tan rectangular cushion, like an oversized bed mattress. It reminded me of the padded rooms in mental institutions in the old days. The sheer size of the padding was hard to appreciate in the poorly lit underground lair, but glinting in the darkness I could see four heavy chains hanging from the top. They were anchored to four giant steel hooks hanging from the ceiling above the padded wall. Even in the dark they were hard to miss.

Uh oh. What the hell are those for?

"Paul... This is... a lot..." I managed to stammer.

He walked to the couch and casually took a seat next to Maryanne. She hadn't said anything since the freezer had revealed itself as a creepy dungeon — maybe this was all new to her, too. Maybe I wasn't the only one trying to keep my composure.

"Well, Rick, things aren't always what they seem," he said calmly.

What does he mean?

Paul pulled a cigarette from the pack in his pants pocket, lit it, and took a deep drag before he continued.

"There are things in this world that are not natural. Not human."

Not human?

"Remember that girl from this morning? The one talking with Christo?"

"Of course. The blonde in the dress. How could I forget her?" That wasn't possible.

"Of course you'd remember the girl in the dress..." Maryanne added with a dramatic eyeroll.

Paul took another drag on his cigarette and I watched the tobacco burn the paper as he inhaled.

"I know this is a lot to take in, but there are creatures out there that aren't human. And they're killing people. And ever since that woman appeared more and more weird shit's been going down. I know you just saw her for the first time this morning, but she's been around for a few weeks. Always with Christo."

Creatures...? Killing people?

In my most deadpan tone I said, "There are non-human creatures going around killing people." I had no right to be skeptical given my surroundings, but I was a cynic at heart. In response, Paul took a final drag then stubbed out the cigarette in the palm of his hand. I saw the ember make contact with his skin, and he didn't even flinch.

"Yes, Rick. Vampires..." He stared at me waiting for my response but I really didn't have one.

Now I know he's gone crazy...

"You expect me to believe that there are mythical

creatures of the night killing people? Come on, man...Vampires?" I was in a secret lair after having seen the corpse of my murdered boss earlier in the day, but still my shit attitude was reigning supreme. I'm not sure what I expected from Paul and Maryanne — a GOTCHA moment, I guess — but I couldn't seem to shut my mouth or justify me being such an asshole.

Paul raised his eyebrows and looked at Maryanne.

"Rick, you can believe what you want. We're just trying to help," he said coolly.

Come on, Paul.

"Help? By dragging me down some hidden stairs to the world's scariest basement and talking to me about supernatural creatures?" I shot Paul and Maryanne my most incredulous look. They were seated together on the mangled couch, unfazed by my vaudevillian doubt. Of the three of us, I was, admittedly, acting the least sane.

Paul stood up and, in the blink of an eye, was directly in front of me, his face only an inch from mine.

"Well, Rick, I'm sure you saw the chains on the padded wall over there," he growled at me.

Those chains? I looked at them again and then back at Paul.

"Yeah, I saw the chains, Paul. I'm not blind," I snapped back realizing that I was probably being too harsh. But I was so scared of all the unknowns.

"They were mine. I needed them to stay safe. Once a month, during a full moon..."

Yikes.

"Look, man. What you do with your free time is your business, okay? I'm not sure I want to know."

Paul walked over to the padded wall and looked up at a crescent-shaped window near the ceiling — the only window in the room. "I'm a wolf," he said calmly. "I mean, technically, I'm a werewolf." *Half-man, half-dog, all crazy.*

"You're. A. Werewolf. Like with the teeth, and claws, and matted fur?"

Paul has more imagination than I thought. And if this is a joke, he's certainly committed...

"Yes, Rick, a werewolf. I used to have to chain myself up to that padded wall every time there was a full moon. Until Maryanne helped," Paul said, lightly touching the sapphire jewel hanging from his neck.

That damn necklace.

"Helped? Helped how? How the hell do you *HELP a WEREWOLF?*" I asked, still being snotty. Neither Paul nor Maryanne, were impressed with the aggressive air quotes I'd added to my nay-saying.

Maryanne was still seated on the couch, though Paul's giant frame was blocking most of my field of vision, so her voice seemed disembodied when she answered. "I put a simple spell on the necklace, so as long as Paul has it on, he can better remain in control. The animal has a harder time taking over."

"So the necklace stops you from changing." I said flatly.

"No, not really. It allows me to change whenever I want to, instead of being forced." Paul took a step back from me, and lit another cigarette. "And it gives me more control while I'm changed. I used to go through the change every full moon, and would have no idea of what I did while all wolfed up." He took another drag. "Luckily, Maryanne could help."

I sighed deeply. I was exhausted; my brain was so fuzzy that I was starting to get on board with the fantasy. "How was

Maryanne able to help you, exactly?" I asked earnestly.

Maryanne looked at me with her dark, gentle eyes that glinted and winked from the darkness. "I'm a witch," she said, staring at me. She twitched her eye and a small fireball shot from Paul's cigarette and then disintegrated into the air.

"Damn it, Maryanne!" Paul jumped. "You know I hate it when you do that!"

She giggled. "Just wait, Rick — I'm good for more than just parlor tricks."

I wish she would teach me a few tricks...

My mind was always in the gutter, but Maryanne looked strangely alluring; I hadn't thought of her like this before. But in that dark grotto, with the smoke from Paul's cigarette curling in the air, I saw her differently. Sexually. I wanted to take her on the couch right in front of Paul and have him watch.

"I first discovered that I was different when I was thirteen. I didn't know how, but I was able to hear some people's thoughts if they were close enough." She went on to explain. "But that was just the beginning. My powers only grew from there. Watch."

She waved her hand and a small wooden chair went flying by my head, nearly hitting me and crashing into the padded wall. She raised her hands up and the whole couch began to levitate off of the ground! Maryanne lowered her hands slowly and set the couch back down, landing it gently.

Okay, that is pretty cool.

My feeling of being afraid quickly morphed into amazement. I was in awe.

"It wasn't until I turned sixteen that my grandmother explained to me what I was. I thought I was just a really strange kid. So, once I found out about Paul's secret, I was able to figure out a way for him to control his gift."

That's quite the gift. I wish that I had a gift.

"Right. Got it. You're a werewolf, and you're a witch," I stated, pointing to each of them. They both nodded. My deadpan comedy routine had fallen flat and now I was simply parroting information.

"Yes," Paul answered from the dark. "Now that you know, we really need to get going."

"Where are we going this time?" I asked, fearful of the answer — the last time he'd said that we ended up here, in a basement, brimming with the paranormal.

Maryanne stood up and said in a comforting voice, "We need to go home, and you need to get some sleep. You've had a day." Her words were remarkably effective, and I immediately felt calmer.

"Yep, she's right, Rick. You've had one hell of a day. And this really is a lot to think about, I know."

Duh. What's next, Paul? Zombies? Ghosts? The Tooth Fairy?

My doubt wasn't completely gone, but at least they hadn't killed me. If they had dragged me into this basement just to play a werewolf/witch prank, it was working. If they hadn't, well, then I suppose I felt different — better, safer — knowing I had a witch and a werewolf on my side. I hoped they were, anyway.

Chapter Five

It was nearly morning by the time I managed to limp into my apartment. For the next three days I did nothing but sleep, eat, think, and sleep some more. On the morning of the fourth day, I finally got up. I was struggling with coming to terms with the supernatural being real, and had hoped that three days asleep would somehow prove it was all just a dream. It wasn't, and I had to figure out what I was going to do. I had missed work and was unsure if I still had a job.

My apartment was dark and spare, just like always. I got up from the recliner — my erstwhile excuse for a bed the past few nights — and made my way to the fridge.

God, I'm hungry. Maybe there's something in the fridge that's still good.

Wrong. The fridge was bare and so were my cupboards. I was left with no choice but to leave my apartment to find some food. I opened the curtains and looked out the window to see if the sun was up or down because I had no idea what time it was. I could see the street lights shining and people standing on the darkened corners out front of my apartment building.

Great. I have to walk to the store in the middle of the night to get food.

I probably wasn't going to starve, but I was ravenous after subsisting on sleep for three days. My knee was still throbbing, but I pushed through the pain and got my shoes on to hobble down four flights of stairs to the street. The wan streetlights did not look happy to see me. I rested against a large dumpster to give my knee a break for a moment before hobbling into the night. I passed two women wearing slutty, tattered outfits, who waved me over to them, trying to earn the night's take from a pathetic john. Probably some guy a lot like myself.

Sorry, ladies. As much as I would love to keep you in business, this guy is broke.

As I limped along, I kept thinking about my underground meeting with Paul and Maryanne a few days before. Could vampires and werewolves actually exist? How could you tell if someone was a vampire or werewolf? When I passed an alleyway and saw a homeless man digging through bags of trash for food, I wondered, *What if he's a vampire? Or a werewolf? What if he tries to kill me? Would I be able to fight him off? No way.* Considering the fact that the supernatural had undoubtedly expanded my mind, all I could see were potential enemies.

About five blocks from my apartment, or, halfway to the store, I noticed something in the cemetery to my right. Normally I would never go near something that creepy, especially at night, but something was drawing me in — a light fog on the ground leading directly into the heart of the cemetery. I felt compelled to follow the fog, and couldn't resist even though every human instinct was telling me not to.

The cemetery was pitch black — the moon sat low on the horizon so the towering skyscrapers blocked nearly all its light — so I couldn't make out any of the names as I passed the tombstones, marking grave after grave. I had no idea where I was going, but could feel myself moving with some unknown purpose.

I continued to follow the fog, then I saw it. A small wooden slat sticking out of the ground with a familiar name stamped on it. Laura Spilkotton, my recently deceased, pain-in-the-ass boss.

Wow. She's really dead.

The thought hadn't really had time to sink in since I'd been asleep for three days, so the wooden slat was a shock. I assumed she must have just been buried as the grave was very disheveled. The dirt was rounded with uneven gravel placed on top of it, almost like a small pitcher's mound. And the wooden sign with her name on it stuck in the ground was an obvious placeholder for where her tombstone would eventually be placed.

I wonder what it will say? Here lies Laura. Beloved boss, and whore. My thoughts of the deceased were not very pleasant, but unfortunately, were based on my many experiences.

It didn't look like many people attended her services given the lack of floral arrangements. But I guess if you act awful to everyone in your life, people will judge that you're not worth saying goodbye to once your life has ended.

I was still deep in thought, and a lonely raccoon was scurrying past Laura's grave, when the ground began to violently shake. New York was not known for earthquakes, so I had no idea what was happening. Pebbles and bits of gravel were vibrating and rolling down the mound of dirt over Laura's grave. The raccoon ran behind a neighboring tombstone to try to escape but there was no avoiding the quaking earth.

The once-clear night sky was now filled with clouds. I wanted to scamper and hide like the raccoon, but I felt welded to that spot. There was a loud crash of thunder, and then another. And another. Over and over again the thunder crashed, each time louder than the time before so that the air was vibrating from the repeated, deafening claps. The hairs on my arms and neck stood straight out, as if reaching into the night to escape my body.

During a momentary break in the thunder, a single bolt of lightning came forking down from the sky and struck the middle of Laura's grave not ten feet from where I was standing. As the lightning hit the ground, the wooden sign sparked before bursting in a flash that lit up the cemetery like fireworks on the Fourth of July.

The ground began to shake even harder. I could see the raccoon still cowering behind the tombstone, trapped. I watched the mist that had lured me into the cemetery thicken into fog and creep between the headstones, obscuring the ground. It was headed straight for Laura's grave.

What the hell? What is all this?

Another bolt of lightning struck her grave in the same place as before. Bolts, one after another, cut through the fog to strike the grave. After only a moment, the bolts of lightning turned into a solid beam shooting down from the skyline. I had never seen anything so scary, and yet so beautiful.

As if right on cue, I noticed movement in my periphery: Maryanne and Paul were walking purposefully into the cemetery, headed directly towards Laura's grave, and me.

"What the hell, you two!?" I shouted.

Maryanne stopped in front of the lightning-filled grave to kneel. She began to chant: *"Even though you're dead below. There's so much more to you I know. So, rise on up out of this grave. Forever more you'll be my slave."*

She finished, but nothing happened. Just more fog.

"What the hell is going on here, Paul? Why are you here? Did you two know Laura?" I asked in an urgent whisper. Paul grabbed my hand and held it gently like I was a small child. Apparently, he could tell I was terrified and even more confused.

"Just watch, Rick. I know you're scared. You've been given a lot to digest over the past few days, but I need you to trust me. I promise that you are safe here with us. Nothing will happen to you," he reassured me in soothing tones.

A bolt of lightning came down directly in front of Maryanne, just missing her as it struck. But she didn't move a muscle, or even flinch. She remained perfectly still kneeling in the dirt, apparently oblivious to the lightning. Again, she chanted in front of the grave.

"Even though you're dead below. There's so much more to you I know. So rise on up out of this grave. Forever more you'll be my slave."

The gravesite rumbled in response. Like another small earthquake concentrated over Laura's gravesite.

This shit is too much. I hope to God nothing is going to come crawling out of the ground. I was terrified for my life.

"I'm going to need you to get comfortable with being uncomfortable Rick. Nothing is going to happen to you," Paul said to reassure me.

As quickly as it had started, the lightning stopped. The fog and clouds cleared. The cemetery was dark and still once again — normal, even.

Suddenly, a hand pushed up through the ground in front of Maryanne. Then it wasn't just a hand, but a whole arm erupting from the earth. And after the first arm came the second. Then a bit of hair started pushing up from the dirt — the top of a head.

"Holy shit! Is... is that Laura? Why is Laura coming up from her grave?" I asked, squeezing Paul's hand in fear.

"Well, I think the best way to explain it is that Maryanne resurrected her," he said flatly. Sensing my numbness, he playfully added, "She can do those kinds of things because she's a witch, y'know." I was not interested in Paul's good-natured ribbing; I wanted answers.

Maryanne chimed in, "I told you I was a witch. And I told you that I can do some pretty nifty things." She winked at me.

Nifty? Creepy.

"So... let me get this straight. You resurrected my dead boss, and now she's a fucking zombie?" I shouted, unwilling to believe my own eyes. Laura was standing still, knee-deep in her grave, covered in dirt. The stitching from where her throat had been slit was crusted with mud.

Maryanne got up from her knees and stood by Laura, jauntily resting her arm upon the corpse's shoulder.

I always wondered if zombies were real.

"She's not a zombie," Maryanne said while gesturing to Laura's grisly throat. "I wasn't sure this was going to work, but when you said her throat had been slit, and there were no bite marks, I was fairly confident."

This is disgusting. I don't want to go near that thing. Fuck! I really don't want to die. I'm not ready to go yet.

I finally let go of Paul's hand and backed away from the reanimated standing in her now former grave. "Should I be worried about it trying to eat me?"

"Rick, she's not going to eat you," Paul said. "I told you that nothing would happen to you and I'm not a liar. Plus, she's not a zombie, so…"

"Well, then, what the fuck is she?" I shouted impatiently.

"She's a Lost One," Maryanne said.

"A what?"

"Rick, she's a Lost One," Paul said. "Let Maryanne explain. Just try to keep an open mind."

"An open mind? Really?"

Why do they expect so much from me?

Maryanne walked over to me and took my hand. "Listen to me, honey."

Honey?

"When a human is killed by a supernatural being, like a vampire or a werewolf, and they aren't TURNED, just MURDERED, their soul gets lost between where it wants to be, and where it needs to be." Maryanne spoke calmly and used her hands to punctuate.

"Like heaven or hell?" I asked, feeling stupid.

"Kind of, but it's more like being stuck between life and death. Like Limbo. Because, technically, she's soulless."

"I never thought Laura had a soul anyways," I muttered. Paul laughed.

"This is no time for jokes, buddy. This is serious," Maryanne chided me. "I guess that was kind of funny, though," she offered. Maryanne could tell that my jokes were just a way to mask how terrified I actually was. "If someone is resurrected, then they belong to the person who brought them back," she stated.

"So you own her?" I asked, motioning to the lifeless woman still supporting Maryanne's casual lean.

"I command her," Maryanne replied. "She will do whatever I ask. Think of her as my puppet. Just a really strong, smelly, dead puppet."

"A resurrected zombie puppet." I said slowly, having never said those words out loud before.

"She's not a zombie," Paul snapped. "She's a Lost One. And she's probably really hungry, Maryanne."

"Probably," Maryanne agreed. "Laura, go find something to eat, but no humans and stay close. Do not leave the cemetery," she ordered the newly-resurrected Dead Laura.

Laura immediately turned to scan the area for food, using her nose to guide her. She ran barefoot into the trees and out of sight so that all we heard were her movements through the trees and thicket. Then, there was a squeal, followed by a gross snap and a crack. Then, silence. After a minute, Laura staggered out from the bushes with a dead squirrel hanging from her mouth. Her shirt was even more ripped and torn than it already had been from her resurrection. Laura had snapped the squirrel's neck and ripped part of its spine out of it with her teeth. Blood spilled from the squirrel and poured directly into her mouth. She tipped her head back and drank the squirrel's blood like it was the last drops of a delicious bowl of soup. After the blood stopped flowing, she sank her teeth into its neck to tear the skin and meat from its bones.

"It looks like she found something to eat," I said. "As disgusting as that is."

"Just be happy that it wasn't you she found to eat," Paul laughed.

"I thought this was no time for jokes," I said casually. Maryanne shot us a stern look to let us know that we needed to stop making jokes.

"Will you two please cut it out? You're embarrassing. We have to figure out what we're going to do with Laura, and find out who killed her, and why."

Paul and I looked at each other. "Better not piss off the witch, Rick," Paul said, poking the bear.

"So, what do we do with the zombie?" I asked. "We can't just walk her back through the city, can we? I mean, don't you think someone would notice a zombie walking around Times Square or Central Park?"

"He's got a point, Maryanne," Paul agreed. "But we have to get her back to the basement; we can keep her down there until we get all of this shit sorted out. And since Lazarus showed up at Rick's work, I'll bet Christo has something to do with all of this."

If we're going to be dealing with Christo, maybe I will get to see her again. My cock stiffened at the thought of her.

Her blonde hair flows over my chest as she sits in my lap. Moving forward and back, and then forward again, pushing me deeper into her with every thrust. Her tight, wet womanhood drips with juices — hers and mine — as I fill her with my love. She moans in my ear as she cums on my lap. I've just exploded inside her, and I can barely move.

Whoa, whoa, whoa. Why am I having a wet dream right now? There is a disgusting zombie in front of me. I literally just saw my dead boss get 'resurrected'. Now is not the time to be thinking about fucking the blonde girl of my dreams

But I didn't just want to fuck her — I wanted to make sweet, passionate love to her. Over and over again. The kind of hot, steamy sex that takes all night and tires us both out completely. The kind neither of us would ever forget. I couldn't figure out why I was so stuck on this woman; I hadn't even met her! Though, I hoped that would change. Sooner rather than later, preferably.

Paul and Maryanne noticed I had zoned out at the mention of Christo.

Paul probably knew what I was thinking about. After all, he was a guy, and it would have been impossible for him not to notice the woman. She was unforgettable.

"Rick, are you all right?" he asked. "You seem kind of distracted, all of a sudden."

"I'm fine, just still really tired. Maybe I need to get some more sleep." I was praying they didn't notice my ever-growing erection. How would I explain a boner in the middle of a cemetery with a witch, a zombie, and a werewolf? The setting wasn't exactly a turn-on.

I'm so sorry, but dead things turn me on.

Umm... eww?

Maybe I was giving my package too much credit. They probably didn't notice anything different at all.

Paul looked at Maryanne. "You find a way to get the Lost One back to the café. I'm gonna head back so sleeping beauty here can get some more rest." Paul and Maryanne both laughed at me. "You can crash at my place tonight. I'll make sure you get back safely with that bum leg of yours." It didn't take much convincing as I didn't want to be alone after what I'd just seen, and my leg was still killing me.

"Thanks, Paul. I appreciate it." I was relieved not to have to go back to my friendless, foodless apartment.

"I'll get Laura back without being seen," Maryanne said confidently.

If she could raise the dead, then she should be able to get a dead puppet across town, I guessed.

Paul started to leave the cemetery and I followed close behind. I assumed that he was walking slower than usual because of my leg. I had never been to his house before, so I had no idea where we were going, or how far, but if it was too much farther, he'd end up carrying me.

The streets were dark and we were the only people on them. Most of the streetlights didn't work in his neighborhood, and the few that did, only flickered. We eventually came to a tall brick building, its walls tagged with all colors of graffiti and the windows smashed and broken. Paul pulled a key from his pocket and unlocked the almost completely busted door.

"This is home. My apartment is on the third floor," he said, motioning up the stairs.

I took one step onto the first stair when my bad knee twisted. I shouted in pain and fell backwards, smacking my head firmly against the wall before crumpling to the floor. I saw Paul reach to catch me as I fell, then blacked out — the blunt force trauma stunning my already addled head.

Chapter Six

Christo walked over to the sumptuous, red-leather couch that spanned the width of the dark room and sat down gracefully. He was wearing standard black jeans and a maroon button-up shirt underneath his ever-present black leather jacket. He was fastidious and particular about his look; his just-so ensemble let people know he had money, and wasn't afraid of spending it.

Against the opposite wall stood a blonde woman with her back turned. She was statuesquely perched on a small, circular, blue carpet in front of a marble counter. From a clear crystal decanter, she poured a dark red liquid into two delicate glasses — one for her, one for the ancient, rich Italian bastard, Christo.

Look at that wine... God, I'm thirsty.

She carried the glasses to the couch but it wasn't until she was right next to Christo that her face came into view.

Oh, my god. It's her. The blonde from Paul's Café — the angel of my dreams... Maybe this is a dream? It feels like a dream, but one someone else is having. Why am I seeing this shit? God, I'd love to be with her.

The woman sat down next to Christo and handed him one of the crystal cups. He tipped his head back as he emptied the glass in two gulps, clearly enjoying every drop of the mystery beverage.

"That's the best blood I've had all week, Lizzie," he said

as he held the now-empty glass above his head, and the last drop of blood trickled from the glass and down Christo's chin. Lizzie leaned in and licked it off, running her tongue slowly across his face.

"Delicious," she said, grinning.

More blood. Great. Why are they drinking it?

"Yeah, you can tell it's fresh," she said, taking a sip from her own goblet. "But I think we have some other business to attend to," she purred as she leaned over Christo to set her glass on the end table next to the couch.

"We sure do," he mumbled as he started kissing her neck. He slid his hand around her shoulder and slowly reached down her back to give her ass a firm squeeze.

No! Ugh. Stop! Don't touch her! Get your fucking hands off of her!

Lizzie was smiling and kissed him back. As they embraced, Christo unzipped the back of her dress and slipped it off her tight body, leaving her standing before him in her bra and underwear.

Put her dress back on, you piece of shit. Please. Please! Why am I seeing this?! How am I seeing this?

"What's the rush?" she asked coquettishly. "You can't be that horny, can you? I just let you have me a few days ago." She was straddling him and running her hand along his thigh before grabbing his cock through his pants. She could feel him bulging beneath her.

"Well, I guess you can be that horny," Lizzie remarked as she rubbed his rock-hard cock through his pants with slow, tight strokes. Christo smiled.

"What can I say? You know how to please me. So, let's get to it." Lizzie's fingers continued to play around his zipper.

"Or maybe you'd prefer to tease me for the rest of the night," he growled. Lizzie unzipped his pants to unloose his massive bulge and paused a moment to close her fingers around his member and feel it throb; his girth was undeniable, and Lizzie was impressed all over again. She sat back as she continued to gently tug.

"We're getting there. But this time I don't want your cash. I don't need your money, Christo."

Damn it. I guess she is a prostitute… It is very unsettling seeing her with this asshole.

Christo's head had been tilted back, and his eyes closed as she walked her fingers around his waist, but with the mention of money he looked at her in confusion.

"If you don't want money, what do you want? You have everything else already: strength and speed. And immortality." His confusion quickly morphed into arrogant impatience. "You will live forever. As long as you don't get yourself killed, you're practically indestructible. Be grateful, toots." He relaxed a little under her touch and said smoothly, "Now, me? I'm a god, honey. I'm over a thousand years old and I can't be killed. I do what I want and nobody fucks with me."

Lizzie untucked his shirt from his unzipped pants and started kissing his waist. She looked up at him and could tell he was enjoying all the attention she was giving him. Almost as much as he was enjoying scolding her. She continued to kiss and lick.

"I want information," she mumbled into his flesh. Christo laughed out loud.

"What could possibly interest you?" he asked disdainfully. Lizzie stopped kissing him and sat up to stare at him intently. Christo flashed his fangs and roared at her, his organ jutting straight out from his body.

"Fine! Tell my dick what the fuck it is you want to know," he ordered.

She smiled and started unbuttoning his shirt as she slowly rocked her hips forward and back along his thighs. With each motion his eyes rolled back and he grunted.

Jesus. Get off him... I'll kill you, Christo — you piece of shit. Leave her alone!

Her questions were punctuated by their shared grunts. "Why are you having Lazarus murder innocent people?" She rocked forward again. "And don't try to tell me he didn't do it." Christo grunted. "Remember, I might not be as old or strong as you, but I'm still a vampire." She gasped as their hips bucked in unison. "And I know you. And I know humans — humans aren't doing these attacks..." Christo let out a guttural moan. "And as far as I know, we're the only vampires in the city," she whispered. Christo's body involuntarily tensed so she pressed, "We are the only ones here, right, Christo?" She stopped rocking and stared at him.

So, vampires are real. There are actual vampires, and they're killing people... God, this is crazy... Did Lazarus kill Laura?

"Attacks? Have there been others?" Christo joked unconvincingly. She was still staring at him, studying him, then he scowled.

Christo grabbed a handful of Lizzie's hair and muscled her head back down towards his cock.

"Open your mouth," he demanded quietly. "I'll tell you what you want to know. But you're gonna have to suck hard, and deep." He tightened his grip on her blonde hair. "Do we understand each other?"

No. No, no! Stop! Don't make her do that! She doesn't want to do that. Why can't I turn off this nightmare porn?!

"I'm waiting," he hissed.

Lizzie sat for a moment with her open mouth poised over his engorged cock. She met Christo's gaze and then put all of his erection into her mouth with one gulp. She rubbed each side of his shaft with her tongue, and then around the tip. Christo moaned, and Lizzie sucked harder. Faster. She scratched the sides of his cock with her fangs and she could feel his whole, thousand-year-old body quiver. She could taste his blood. She bobbed her head up and down and heard him gasp, and then roar. His hips arched forward as he burst in her mouth and his seed shot down her throat. She swallowed every drop of him, and kept her fangs around his member even after he was spent, resting her head on his belly. He untangled his fingers from her hair and leaned back, satisfied.

"I feel much better. Like a newborn vampire. I feel like I could take on the world." Christo sighed, "Nobody sucks a cock quite like you, my dear. So thank you." She narrowed her eyes as she stared him down. "I guess I should hold up my end of the bargain now," he said with a smirk.

Lizzie laughed. "The only things you know how to hold up are two-bit mobsters, and your dick," she said playfully while stepping into her dress.

She turned and Christo zipped it up, before he pulled his pants up and re-tucked his shirt in one swift motion.

"Well, to be honest, honey, the only person I've killed… recently… is Laura. I'm not talking about the ten or twenty random nobodies I ate because I was hungry. A guy's gotta eat, after all." Christo smoothed back his white hair with his giant hands. "And as for Laura, I didn't really do that. I'd asked

Lazarus to kill her, but he was resistant, for some reason. So I compelled him to slit her throat," he said casually. "I guess next time I should be a little more specific, because the dumb fuck killed her in her office. Apparently, there were other people there, but Lazarus said there weren't any issues that needed to be handled."

Lizzie poured another glass of blood from the decanter and sipped it slowly.

"But why kill her? What's the angle? I mean godDa.m.N, Christo, I thought we were supposed to stay UNDER the radar."

Christo turned to the wall of windows to his left and looked into the night as he spoke. "What is the reason for killing a human, Lizzie? Other than for eating, I mean. Or for the sport of it," Christo chuckled.

"Christo!" Lizzie was tired of his melodramatic stalling. "Stop playing. Why are you killing innocent people?"

Christo took a dramatic sigh before shaking his head and chuckling condescendingly. "Oh, Lizzie, don't be stupid. What the hell do you think happened? Laura found out about us. I don't know how, but she found out that Lazarus and I aren't human, so she had to die. You know the rules. She might have even known about you, doll," he purred as he snatched her glass of blood from her hand and drained it. "But what do I care? I can't be killed."

"So, does anyone else know about us?" she asked urgently. "Did Laura know about me? God damn it Christo!" she shouted. "I really like this city, and I don't want to have to leave it because you can't stop killing people!"

"Relax. I don't think any other humans know about us."

Lizzie paused to study Christo's expression before asking

in a serious voice, "What exactly does that mean? That no other HUMANS know about us... What aren't you telling me?"

"I mean that no other *humans* know about us..." He turned from her and mumbled into the window. "But something does..." With that, she turned him back towards her by grabbing his shoulder and sinking her nails into him.

"What the fuck are you talking about? Something? What the hell does that even mean? What is something?"

He took another drink from her glass and swallowed hard. He was obviously stalling.

With a sigh he said, "I have reason to believe that vampires are not the only supernatural creatures in New York."

Lizzie's brow furrowed in confusion and anger. "And what would make you think that?" she asked.

"A few weeks ago, I saw a man alone in the park behind some trees." He paused.

"Aaaand?" she offered.

"Don't be a bitch — I saw a man, yes. But he was different. He was changing into something... Something big."

"What do you mean... changing?"

"...It was dark, and he was behind some trees... but he changed into something I've never seen. He bent down behind the trees as a human, but when he stood up he was completely different."

Christo thought back to the moment and his expression immediately changed; he looked nervous, like a child alone in the dark.

"Different how?" Lizzie asked, noticing the shift in his composure.

"Well, he was much taller. Seven, eight feet. And it looked

like he was covered in black and grey fur." Christo looked at Lizzie and said, "And his face, I mean, his head was no longer human, but more like an animal."

Lizzie waited for him to continue but Christo seemed stuck in his memory. "What was wrong with his head, Christo?" she asked.

Christo let out a sharp laugh and then yelled, "It was a fucking wolf head!" Christo's supernatural-sized anxiety was making him unstable, and Lizzie worried he might collapse.

"What kind of wolf?" she asked in a calming tone.

"No ordinary wolf. More like the kind from horror stories. Like the ones about our kind. I have been around for a long, long time, Lizzie, and honestly, it gave me nightmares." Christo steadied himself against the window pane. "Huge fangs, big red eyes, and it howled at the moon. It was like nothing I'd seen before. And that noise was nothing like I'd heard before, either. Then it happened."

Lizzie drew in a long breath before she asked, "What happened?" She had never seen Christo be so afraid of anything, which terrified her.

"It looked right at me with its red eyes. Like it *knew* me. I'm pretty sure it knows what I am, at least. I had just fed and was still holding the body, so it definitely saw me eating someone." Christo turned back to the window away from Lizzie, ashamed by his own fear.

"So after it saw you, what happened next?" She needed to know. "Nothing. It ran into the woods, and that was the last I saw of it… It moved really, really fast, and ran on two legs like a human, but I don't think it was. Human, I mean."

Lizzie sat on the couch and breathed in deeply through her nose, and out her mouth as she tried to digest everything she'd just been told.

"This sounds pretty absurd, Christo. I mean, I never believed in anything supernatural... But then I died and was given another chance."

He reached over and took her hand. "I'm really glad you got another chance, Lizzie. I only wish I could have been the one to turn you."

She pulled her hand away. "Thanks, but Richard did just fine. He taught me everything he knew before he disappeared. Then I met you..." Lizzie looked up at him then continued in a stern voice, "But that's not important. We need to focus on this wolf."

The moon emerged from behind the night's clouds and poured bright moonlight into the apartment, lighting the living room. The lines in Christo's ancient face seemed to deepen in the shadows cast against the moonglow.

"It's a full moon tonight," he said, staring out the window.

"This is the problem, Christo," Lizzie said with increasing alarm. "Because if I didn't know any better, I'd say you're talking about a damn werewolf."

Christo let a cruel laugh erupt from his belly. He was manic.

She continued, "Think about everything you've just said, Christo. Put it together, you jackass."

He stopped laughing and became visibly tense before saying to her in a quiet, almost timid voice: "I've never had to deal with a werewolf before, Lizzie. Do we have to kill it? How do we kill it?" His chest rose and fell with a massive sigh before he sat back on the couch, dejected.

Lizzie sat down next to him and leaned back to take another sip from her glass. "Well, according to all the stories, we should start with silver bullets, of course," she said smiling, and only half-joking.

"Silver bullets and werewolves are childhood myths," Christo replied, trying to convince himself.

"Are they?" she countered. "Vampires are childhood myths too, Christo. Yet, here we are."

He knew she was right but he didn't like it. He sulked on the couch as he wondered how they were supposed to find the werewolf and then, more importantly, how they would kill it.

Lizzie finished up her blood and began brainstorming.

"We should set a trap. I don't know how, and I don't know what kind. But we need a trap." Christo rolled his eyes.

"Well, aren't you just full of really helpful ideas?" he said, annoyed. Lizzie bowed her head and lowered her eyes in penitence for disappointing him. Christo could see she was upset, but was unbothered. He tilted her head and firmly held her chin, their red eyes locked onto each other. A single tear ran down Lizzie's cheek and Christo wiped it away with his thumb.

"You're fine, angel. No more tears," he said as he pulled a tissue from his pants pocket. "We'll get Lazarus and then the three of us will learn everything we can about werewolves. We have a month; when the moon is full again, we'll go hunting. Even if it is a werewolf, there isn't a creature alive that would want to fuck with the three of us."

Christo gave Lizzie a kiss on her cheek, then demanded she take a shower. He didn't care who the girl was or what part of her he'd sullied, he always wanted them to clean themselves once he was done. The only times he flouted the shower-after-sex policy were when the girl died in the process, which happened more often than not.

Where is she going?

Lizzie began to disappear. She kept getting farther and farther away and all I wanted was to reach for her. To try to make sense of this mess. I heard her turn on the shower in Christo's bathroom, but I could no longer see her. Then, she was gone. As quickly as she'd appeared. *Where is Christo?* He had disappeared too, and so had his apartment. Everything faded into nothing, and I was left to try to sleep after that horrifying nightmare.

Chapter Seven

I woke completely covered in sweat. My heart was racing, my head was pounding and I had no idea where I was. I knew I was in a bed that wasn't mine, in a bedroom that didn't belong to me. And my knee was still extremely sore. Where the hell was I?

Holy shit. Was that really a dream? It felt so real. I actually thought I was in that room with the gorgeous blonde… I seriously need a fucking CT scan.

I remembered the cemetery, and how strange it was. As my eyes focused and I took some breaths, I remembered I was at Paul's house. Yes. He invited me to his place for the night, and Maryanne was going to the cafe to put the Lost One in the basement. Memories of the night before came flooding back. I remembered tripping up Paul's stairs and whacking my head — I must have passed out as soon as I hit the wall. Paul had tried to catch me, but I fell.

I rubbed the sleep out of my eyes and looked around. The bedroom was dimly lit but the sun was shining bright on my legs and feet through the window to my left. It must have been early in the morning. There was a dresser to the right of the bed, on which a small bowl of gelatinous material and a small cup of orange juice neatly sat. They were the only noteworthy items in the room — everything else was drab and nondescript. It felt like a wooden prison cell.

I sat up slowly when movement caught the corner of my eye — a quick flash like someone had run past the slightly open bedroom door. I'd thought I was alone.

What the hell was that? Maybe it's Paul coming to check on me…

My mind began to wander.

Did all that shit really happen last night at the graveyard? I hope not. I hope to God that it's just crazy dreams or maybe I've been drinking a little too much. Or way too much.

Suddenly, there were a series of loud thuds outside the bedroom, like someone falling down the stairs. I winced as I moved my knee to get out of the bed when the door flew open. I couldn't believe my eyes. I wanted my brain to be lying to me and my vision to be wrong, but there was no mistake: Dead Laura was standing in the doorway.

Her skin was mottled and covered in lesions. There were three metal chains wrapped around her neck. Her face was smeared with dirt and the slash across her throat was bulging and horribly pronounced. Her eyes were red and a trail of black liquid hung from her mouth — likely the blood of the squirrel she'd devoured the night before.

"Aaargh!" I shrieked loudly as I moved to slam the door shut. The door was blocked by one of her undead zombie arms, swinging lifelessly towards me. I threw my whole weight at the door to force it closed, but Dead Laura was pushing against the door from the other side. She was possessed with inhuman strength, and seemed determined to get to me. I knew my strength would only last a few more seconds, and was afraid of what she might do to me.

"Help! Somebody, help me!" I screamed. I was knocked back when Dead Laura forced the door open and moved in on me like her prey, ready to pounce. I was cowering when I heard footsteps, followed by a familiar voice that brought an immediate sense of relief.

"Back up, Laura," Maryanne said as she pushed past Dead Laura to help me to my feet. "Do you remember Rick? He's a friend. You used to work with him. We like Rick, Laura."

Yeah Laura, you like me. Remember? You used to like me way too much.

Dead Laura grunted slightly as if in acknowledgement of Maryanne's gentle reminders that I was a friend. "Just stay calm, Rick, and everything will be just fine. Everything is all right," she said as she petted Dead Laura's head, trying to keep her relaxed.

Ugh, Maryanne. That is disgusting. Don't touch that ugly thing! I certainly wouldn't.

"Maryanne, what the hell? Is… is that Laura, and is she trying to kill me?"

Maryanne sighed at my question and rolled her eyes. "Oh, Rick. She's not trying to kill you, sweetie. Don't you remember me resurrecting her last night? We were at the cemetery and I brought Dead Laura up from her grave. Paul said you fell and hit your head coming up the stairs when you got back — I hope you're all right. He brought you here."

My memories were coming back piecemeal. The cemetery and the fog. The lightning striking the grave. And — what did she call her? — Dead Laura, who had ripped a squirrel apart and eaten it like it was an afternoon snack. I was remembering, but it felt unreal. Like every scene was from a crazy dream. Or, a nightmare that I could not escape.

"So all of that crazy shit actually happened." It was a statement, but I hoped she would hear it as a joke and could reassure me that I was dreaming, and that monsters weren't real.

"I'm afraid so," she said in a calming and reassuring tone. I wondered how any of this could even be possible and was neither calmed, nor reassured.

I took a shaky breath. "So Laura is actually, technically dead. But you resurrected her." I looked to the doorway and the rotting corpse blocking my exit and cried, "I'm seriously freaking the fuck out and I'm sorry, but Dead Laura is not helping!" I was hysterical.

Maryanne placed her hand on my shoulder to calm me down and looked into my eyes. "I understand. Your whole world has been turned completely upside down; I get it, I really do. There's a lot to wrap your head around when you find out about the Other World."

The Other World?

I reluctantly asked, "What exactly do you mean by the Other World?" Dead Laura grunted at the mention of this other world as Maryanne began to explain things to me slowly and calmly. I could tell she wanted me to fully understand what she was saying.

"It's not an actual other planet, Rick. When I say 'Other World,' I am referring to the supernatural side of our plane — the world we live in. Now, usually the supernatural world and the natural world stay completely separate from each other." Maryanne placed her hands far apart to demonstrate. "But sometimes that's not the case. There are cosmic moments when the two worlds kind of brush against each other." She rubbed her hands together. "When the two sides clash, very bad things can happen." Maryanne's hands suddenly burst into flames, as if from friction. "When the two sides clash, people usually end up dying. Like Laura here." She gestured to the zombie, which was still staring at me. In a blink the fire in Maryanne's hands was gone.

Dead Laura? Well, boo-hoo. I was sorry that innocent people died, but it was hard to feel sorry for someone who spent so much of her waking life being a pain in my ass. Sure, she has been turned into a lurching, drooling zombie, but at least she wasn't harassing me any more.

"And, by the way, Laura is completely harmless." Maryanne paused to giggle and wink before adding, "Unless I tell her not to be…" Dead Laura grunted, as if in assent.

I chose to ignore Maryanne's 'joke', and instead tried to get a handle on the facts. "So, this is Paul's house, correct?" I asked, having no memory of anything from after my fall on the stairs the previous night.

"Yes, sir," Maryanne nodded.

Damn! What about work?

I hadn't been back to the office since finding Laura's still-bleeding corpse. A fact sure to please the comically fat detective who I was willing to bet was all too happy to jump to conclusions about why I had completely disappeared right after her throat was slit.

"Maryanne, I really should think about getting to work. I haven't been in a few days and I need to see what Tony has done with the place. You understand. Now that Laura is, well… Dead Laura, I am not entirely sure I still have a job."

I tried to talk about Laura with compassion, to show some respect for the dead, but this was a challenge. In life she'd been abusive, manipulative, and mean. I'm pretty sure she took pride in sexually harassing me, like some inverse scarlet letter. Maybe other guys were into that kind of thing, but it turns out

I'm not like those other guys. And Laura, alive or dead, certainly wasn't for me.

"I'm sure that soda place can get by without you for a few days. I know Paul and I have, well, quite a few things to try to sort out, and that you still need to get used to everything. I'm sure Lightning Pop will manage."

Clearly, she didn't know just how pathetic an office Lightning Pop was. Poor Tony was probably still a mess from Laura's murder, and it wouldn't take much more than two people's absence for the office to grind to a complete halt.

"Plus, you're going to need a few days to heal that leg of yours. And now you're also sporting a head injury," she ribbed, adding insult to my injuries. The throbbing in my head had drowned out the dull ache in my leg so that I had almost forgotten getting run down by a taxi just days before. While this near-death experience, wasn't one I would typically forget, I'd had multiple brushes with death and gore since.

"I guess I can take a few more days off and see if I can get this leg healed up. Maybe I'll get used to some of these supernatural things in the meantime." I didn't really have the energy to argue with her as I knew how persistent Maryanne could be.

She clapped her hands together and bounced up and down in excitement like a child. "Yay!" she shouted. "This will be fun! I'll take care of you and get you better."

Take care of me? What does that mean? Like, give me a sponge bath? The mere thought of Maryanne giving me a sponge bath got me immediately, though mildly, aroused.

"Hey, I have something I want to ask you about at some point," I added trying to be nonchalant, but killing the vibe nonetheless.

"Sure, Rick. You can ask me anything. First, can you help me get Dead Laura downstairs to Paul? Last I knew he was in the kitchen making breakfast."

Paul, whose house we were in, hadn't appeared all morning.

Good thing he's cooking because I'm starving. I hope he's cooking something other than that slop that was next to the bed. Because that shit looked like somebody puked in a bowl and called it oatmeal.

"Umm, I think so," I said, looking at the drooling, grunting, lifeless Laura. "How do we get it downstairs? Do we drag her by her chains?" I really didn't want to touch the zombie.

Maryanne smiled and gently tugged on one of the chains around Dead Laura's neck, who grunted and lurched forward. "We just need to lead her down the stairs. Be careful — just make sure she doesn't fall, or anything," she said to encourage me.

Yeah, we wouldn't want her to get hurt or anything.

I stood still like an idiot.

"Just grab her shoulder and help me guide her," Maryanne said firmly.

Jesus, I have to touch it?

I was less-than-thrilled to grab onto Dead Laura, but quickly realized that I didn't have anyone to trust except Maryanne and Paul. Neither one of them had misled me yet, and they made me feel calm and safe even when using words like 'vampire' and 'supernatural'. And so far, they were the only ones who attempted to make any sense out of my increasingly absurd experiences. But I'd been alone for so long that trusting others felt unnatural. I was playing it cool, but I also knew I didn't have a choice other than to trust. So, I reluctantly and carefully steered Dead Laura by nudging her shoulder. She let out one of her signature grunts.

The three of us managed to make it down the stairs in one piece where we passed through the living room to get to the kitchen. Paul's two-story, third-floor, walk-up apartment was surprisingly small, and clearly lived in. Piles of what I assumed was dirty laundry dotted the floor, around a brown, leather recliner that had a baby-blue, clearly homemade, Afghan draped over it. In the middle of the floor there was a large, emerald-green carpet that matched the one in the basement of the café. Except this one wasn't ripped and torn — it looked brand new.

The large picture window in the front of the living room was covered with curtains that matched the baby-blue Afghan. It looked like Paul had been living there by himself, and that he wasn't one for decorating.

Sheesh, this place could use a woman's touch. Shit, I could use a woman's touch. A certain blonde woman, specifically. I wonder what it would be like to be inside her... To feel her, and have her feel me...

Every time I thought about her, I got an instant erection, and this was no exception. I could feel my jeans tightening around my balls, and if I wasn't careful, I was going to explode in the middle of Paul's living room.

Luckily one look at Dead Laura and: Boom. Erection gone. Like sexual clockwork, my arousal was there one minute, and gone the next.

Paul was in the kitchen, standing in front of the stove in his shorts and a t-shirt. He was wearing an apron that said 'Kiss The Cook' with a pair of oversized red lips underneath. He turned and noticed Maryanne and I guiding Dead Laura, and chuckled at our ridiculous trio. Who wouldn't have?

Thanks. Nice to see you, too.

"Good morning, sleeping beauty," he said, giving me a nod. "How's your head? You took a pretty decent fall last night, getting up the stairs at the front of the building. Are you all right?" He seemed legitimately concerned.

"Christ, I'm feeling it this morning," I responded as I pulled up a chair to the kitchen table to give my leg a rest. "My head definitely hurts, but my leg is in pretty rough shape," I said, now sitting.

The smell of something delicious hung in the air, and it made my stomach rumble violently. Maryanne took a seat and tied Dead Laura's chains to a chair, keeping her on a tight leash.

"Stay," she commanded Dead Laura, like a dog.

"What are you cooking, Paul? Oof, I can't believe how hungry I am," I offered, hopeful that he would take pity and share his grub. I could smell bacon frying, which was making me hungrier.

"I got some pancakes going, and some bacon. Nothin' fancy."

"Perfect. I can't remember the last time I ate…"

It felt like days, but in the past week everything had been kind of a blur. My waking life felt like a nightmare that I couldn't wake from. Except when I thought about her — nothing else mattered when she was in my head. It felt like the world around us stopped.

Paul put two pancakes on a plate and served them to Maryanne. I did my best to remain patient as she cut through them like butter with her fork. Paul must have heard my stomach growling because he gave me three pancakes, and four strips of bacon.

I could get used to this! Most of my meals come out of a fucking can.

"Rick, what did you want to ask me upstairs?" Maryanne asked in between huge bites of buttered pancakes. I was shoving forkfuls into my mouth, too, but she looked much better doing it. I was tearing my pancakes apart like a lion ripping into a gazelle. And gnawing on my bacon like it was muscles and tendons from that same gazelle's freshly broken legs.

"I guess I wanted to ask you — both of you — about the dream I had last night. It was pretty scary." I shoved another bite of bacon into my already-full mouth, and hoped they could still understand me as I masticated.

Paul took a seat and pulled off his apron, exposing his sapphire necklace. "So, why don't you tell us about it?" he said while drowning his pancakes in syrup. I hesitated for just a moment as I wondered if I should try to put my crazy cream into words.

Fuck it. I have nothing to lose.

"I saw Christo. In what I'm assuming was his apartment. But I don't know. Anyways, he wasn't alone — he had company…" Maryanne forced a small piece of pancake into Dead Laura's mouth and she grunted as she swallowed it whole.

"Who was with him?" Maryanne asked.

I was excited to learn what they knew about the woman, but was hoping I could do so without an immediate, full-blown erection. "It was the same blonde woman who was with him at your café the other day." I paused because I didn't want them thinking I was crazy, but quickly realized we were way past that.

"So, the two of them were in his apartment and they were talking about things. Like, things that you normally don't hear people talking about."

Paul and Maryanne shared a look before he asked, "What kinds of things were they discussing?"

"Well, Paul. Vampires... And they were drinking something that looked a lot like blood." I shoveled more bacon into my mouth.

I must sound like I belong in the nuthouse...

"When they were sitting on the couch, they were talking about something that they both seemed to be really afraid of," I added.

"Well, that can't be right. Christo isn't afraid of anything," Maryanne said. "He's an immortal, after all."

"Well, in this crazy little dream of mine, it sounded like they were pretty afraid of werewolves..." I said reluctantly.

Paul got up from the table and walked to the kitchen window.

Maryanne cut in to offer, "Well, it sounds like you had a pretty intense dream!"

"Stop, Maryanne," Paul said while staring out the window. "It's high time someone found our secrets out. And for some reason, the supernatural world really wants to include Rick. So, let's include him." Maryanne nodded in solemn agreement.

"I told you in the basement that I am a witch." Maryanne looked me dead in the eyes. "But I'm not a regular witch."

Regular witch? What is a regular witch?

"Not a regular witch," I repeated back to her.

"I'm a Bogarden. My full name is Maryanne Bogarden Prescott. The Bogarden bloodline has produced some of the strongest witches that have ever existed. Our magic cannot be taught — you have to be born with it." She let the weight of her words hang over the breakfast table.

I was trying to fit the pieces of the puzzle together. "I believed that you were a witch when you brought back Dead Laura. But really, you're the latest super-powerful witch in a long line of even more powerful witches?" I asked, to confirm.

"Extremely powerful witches," Paul added.

Why has he been so quiet through most of this conversation? Is there something more he's not telling me?

"Right. And you?" I questioned as I turned to Paul. He stared blankly at me as he gripped his necklace. I could sense that there was something he wasn't telling me.

"Well, Rick," he said slowly. "You know that my name is Paul…" He raised his eyebrows at me.

"Yeah, Paul. But I guess I've never heard your last name. It's always just been Paul." He stood still as I returned his blank stare.

"I have a second name. It's Wolvenside…"

Wolvenside? Oh, lord.

"Maryanne's not the only one here with a secret past, Rick. I told you; I'm a wolf. Cursed by the moon. Or, I was until Maryanne rescued me." Paul looked at her with gratitude.

Paul sat back down and took off his necklace and set it on the table in front of me. I had never seen anything so blue and beautiful — it made the ocean look ugly.

"You see, when I met Maryanne, I was a new werewolf. I wasn't able to control the change," he continued. "I was born with this curse, but the first change didn't come until I was sixteen. Maryanne met me when I was eighteen. It had been two years of me being unable to control the wolf, unable to control myself. She saw my pain and offered to help. She told me she could help me control the wolf, and therefore control the change." Paul sighed.

"So, you—" I pointed to Maryanne, "help him?" I asked while gesturing toward Paul. "How?" Paul was huge and Maryanne was dainty. I couldn't really understand what she could do for him that he couldn't do himself, and hoped they would continue to explain things to me as if to a small child. I had never claimed to be an intellectual, but this was making me feel really dumb.

"Usually, werewolves have to change whenever the moon is full. The process is extremely slow and painful, and once the transformation is complete, the wolf takes over completely. At that point the human is no longer there," Paul explained seriously.

"What happens when you are a wolf? Do you hunt for food? Or... people?" I asked.

Or maybe you lick yourself just because you can?

"You lose control over your human nature. You literally become a hungry, horny, pissed-off wolf. You'll rip apart anything that stands in your way: Mom, child, dog, bear. It doesn't matter. Whatever crosses your path, you will destroy. You crave the sound of cracking bones and the taste of blood and the ripping of flesh." He said all this slowly while staring at me.

"Okay, so, you're dangerous. But how did Maryanne help you?" I was being pushy, but I wanted to know. "What did she do? Did she stop you from changing?" I wanted more information.

"No, all I did was give him that pretty blue necklace," she answered.

"She did more than that," Paul said, laughing a little. "She enchanted this sapphire so that as long as I wear it, I no longer have to change on full moons. So now when I do change — when I choose to change — it's painless and instantaneous. And the best part is that when I'm transformed, I maintain complete control of the wolf. It's made all the difference; I'm no longer a killing machine. I mean, unless I have to be..."

What set of circumstances would make Paul have to be a killing machine? Do I even want to know?

"So, Maryanne basically made it so you can control the wolf, and so you don't have to change?" I parroted, hoping I'd gotten the gist.

"Right," Paul said. "I owe her everything. She gave me my freedom." He looked at Maryanne intently before adding, "She gave me my life back."

"Oh, don't be silly. Your friendship and protection are enough for me."

Maryanne smiled.

I knew that Paul and Maryanne were close, but it wasn't until that moment that I realized just how close they really were. They weren't a couple. And they weren't fucking, as far as I knew. But they were clearly family, and looked out for each other, because that's what family does.

If only I had a family like that.

Paul grabbed the now empty plates and put them in the sink. Maryanne gave the end of the pancakes to Dead Laura, which she accepted with yet another grunt. My knee was still bothering me, but I got up and wiped down the kitchen table with a rag that was on the counter, eager to earn my keep.

"We should get the café opened up soon, Maryanne," Paul said over the clink of the soapy dishes he was washing in the sink.

"Yeah, I'm going to keep Dead Laura in your doggy den in the basement," she laughed.

"Of course you are. Why wouldn't you?" Paul responded, jovially. "You gonna spend the day with us, Rick?"

What else am I going to do? I could have gone home, but there was nothing for me there. Certainly, no makeshift family members, supernatural or otherwise.

"Yeah, I'll hang out. I've got nowhere else to be really. I can help you out with the café, if you want," I added hopefully. It's not like I was going to hobble to Lightning Pop. "And I guess we have to get Dead Laura back to the café, somehow? I don't really want to touch her again, but I'm here, and I'll help you out."

It really is the least I can do; if they're trusting me with their secrets, I can help out with Dead Laura.

The four of us — a powerful witch, a latent werewolf, an undead employer, and a guy with a bump on his head and a bum leg — were on our way to Paul's Café. I could tell life was going to be different for me from now on. I had been exposed to a world full of supernatural beings: zombies, werewolves, vampires. But was that all? What if the list was never-ending? What if there was no end to the variety of fantastical creatures that were, in fact, real? I was trying to adjust on the fly, but the learning curve was steep. Steeper even than the rickety flight of stairs I'd fallen down the night before.

Chapter Eight

The sun was beating down on the rusted roof of Paul's rusted Chevy Impala. I was buckled into the backseat alongside Dead Laura. Even though I was seated next to a drooling, grunting zombie, imminent death seemed more likely from Paul's driving — I was sure we were going to pop a tire every time he whipped his aging Chevy around a corner. I was somewhat comforted by Maryanne's presence, though; if I was about to be killed in a car accident at least she could witch me back to life. Not to mention that Dead Laura needed supervision that I was not in the mood to provide.

My whole world had changed in the past week. Everything I thought was, wasn't. And the inverse: Everything I thought wasn't, was. Apparently, there was a supernatural world that existed all around me that was full of vampires, werewolves, and zombies. I didn't know what else was possible and was scared to even imagine. In the week since I had seen her that first time in the café, everything had changed.

...Lizzie...? Christo called her Lizzie in that horrible nightmare.

The beautiful girl I couldn't stop thinking about — Lizzie — seemed right in the middle of everything, and I wasn't convinced this was simply coincidental. She looked normal, but I was almost positive she wasn't. In my dream she and Christo were blood-sucking vampires, and maybe there was something to that. After all, it was the first time I had ever dreamt of soulless creatures of the night.

Damn, I'd give anything to have her bite me... suck on my neck... Or any part of me she could get her lips around...

"Hey, Maryanne. Are we just hoping that nobody notices there's a zombie in this car?" I asked as I gestured to my undead seatmate. The zombie grunted at my question. "Oh, sorry; Dead Laura." In recognition of my correction, she brushed against me and dripped what looked like a dark mixture of drool and blood on my shoulder. I shuddered. On top of everything else, I now had to mind my manners to the undead when all I wanted was to get away from her.

Even dead, she still likes me. Great. Just great.

Maryanne turned to answer from the front seat, "I put a complete coverage spell on her back at Paul's house, so, basically, she's only visible to me, you, and Paul."

Now the zombie is invisible? I'm never gonna get used to all of this supernatural shit.

"Well, that's good, I guess. We wouldn't want Paul to lose business just because there's a goddamn zombie running around the café terrorizing people." I chuckled slightly as Paul turned sharply around another corner and slammed on the breaks. I slammed up against Dead Laura and immediately stopped laughing to instead focus on surviving Paul's driving.

"We're here!" Paul said cheerfully. He looked to each of us — his carload of misfits — to make sure that we were all in one piece. "Everybody out! Last stop, Paul's Café!" he said in a singsong voice, as if he were the tour-guide on a tour of one-star cafes in NYC.

I'm no tourist, pal, but I'm more than ready to get out of this damn deathtrap you call a car.

"Rick, can you help me get Laura inside to the basement?" Maryanne asked, giggling. She knew how uncomfortable I was with Dead Laura, and seemed to enjoy requesting my help.

"Yeah, Rick. Help her get Dead Laura downstairs and I'll go ahead and get the place opened up." I was the newbie so I was put on zombie duty, from what I could tell. Maryanne didn't seem to mind my help, though.

Paul locked his car door and started toward the café. He paused a few feet in front of the oak-stained double doors. "The lights are on," he said. "But I know I turned 'em off last night." He walked around the side of the building and peered in through the tinted windows by cupping his hands to his face, and his face to the glass.

"Shit. There's somebody in my café..." he hissed.

"Wha — urgh! — What do you mean?" I asked as Maryanne and I held onto a struggling Dead Laura's chains.

"I mean there is someone sitting in my goddamn café who I didn't ask to be there!" Paul was evidently not used to dealing with strangers in his place, and was getting visibly angrier with each passing second.

Who the hell breaks into a café?

Maryanne shot me a look before suggesting, "Let's put Dead Laura back in the car for a few minutes so that the three of us can go see who popped in for a visit. Together." She looked at Paul, who was quickly losing his cool.

The three of us? What if it's somebody dangerous? Or someTHING?

I don't even know how to defend myself... I think I'd rather take my chances with the zombie in the car.

Maryanne gently pushed on Dead Laura's head to get her

back in the car, then I stuffed the rest of her in from behind her.

"Oof. That should do it. STAY," she said to Dead Laura as she shut the door in the zombie's face. "Let's go see who's here." Maryanne seemed all too excited about an intruder. So much so that there was no way I was going to convince her that we should proceed cautiously. Logically. Sanely. Paul faced the doors and Maryanne stood directly behind him. I tried to position myself behind them both so if there was any kind of threat, they'd have to deal with Paul and Maryanne first.

Why does this shit keep happening? And why does it keep happening TO ME?

Paul pushed gently on the double-doors and they slowly swung open. We were greeted by the smell of freshly-brewed coffee. Paul's coffee. No question; he served a Colombian blend, with the slightest hint of dark chocolate. You could only get it at Paul's.

Maryanne and Paul stepped over the threshold and then stopped where they stood. I was behind them like a shielded puppy, but pushed forward through them to see who, or what had stopped them in their tracks. I half assumed that whatever they saw was not overly dangerous since both of them were just standing still, not taking any actions. But the other half assumption was that whatever it was, was so dangerous that they were frozen in fear. Good thing I had a lifetime's worth of playing the odds, however poorly.

Then, standing between Paul and Maryanne, I was also stopped in my tracks. I couldn't believe my eyes. Was I daydreaming? It wasn't an intruder, per se. It wasn't anything hostile, so far as I knew.

Is... Is that...? No way! Oh. My. God.

Lizzie was sitting at a table alone. Even with her back to us we could tell she was sipping from a cup of Paul's coffee. She was wearing a bright red sweater, and what looked like dark, blue jeans. Even in the moment I hoped they were tight. She was perched on one of Paul's old wooden chairs, her smooth blonde hair flowing past her shoulders and covering the top half of the back of the old chair. Her sweater had risen up just enough to expose the smooth skin of her lower back. Even from behind I knew she was flawless. Perfect.

She even looks gorgeous from the back. My dream girl. Is this my chance to finally talk to her…? What would I even say?

"Well, good morning, everyone," she said calmly as she turned around to face us. As she turned her body, her bright red sweater accentuated her beautiful set of breasts, which now pointed directly at me.

Well, hello there. Aren't you a sight for sore eyes…

Paul made a small growl under his breath.

Did he just growl at her? What a chump. You can't take werewolves anywhere, apparently.

He clenched one fist at his side as he pointed at her with his other hand. His fingernails began to slowly extend, growing over the tips of his fingers to become claws. Razor-sharp, animalistic claws. Clearly, he wasn't worried about exposing his secret, inner-wolf to her.

Damn, what's he gonna do with those? Please don't slice up the girl of my dreams Those talons look really sharp.

"The next words outta your mouth had best be an explanation as to why the hell you broke into my place," he growled. To drive his point home, he added, "Or we're gonna have a serious issue here."

Lizzie set her cup on the coffee-ring-stained table and

smiled back at him.

"Now, now. There's no reason for claws here. Be a good dog. I'm not here for a fight," she purred. Paul growled again, louder, but retracted his claws as he lowered his arm.

"Ugh. Vampires are always looking for a fight," Maryanne added, spitefully. "That's what you do best. Fight things, then kill them." She frowned and crossed her arms over her chest.

Please shut up, Maryanne. Don't antagonize this gorgeous girl... Errr, vampire, I suppose.

"I promise you that I am not here to harm anyone, or cause any problems for you three. Truly. I mean, clearly, I'm out numbered." The gorgeous blonde looked at each of us, up and down, obviously finding us a non-threat. "You don't have to be wearing a pointy hat and a long black robe for me to recognize you as a witch," Lizzie said coolly, nodding to Maryanne. She then turned to Paul. "And you: You're obviously a werewolf. I could smell you from three miles away. There's no reason to threaten me with your claws. Trust me, your rotten dog's breath and fleas gave you away. Plus, I saw you scratching yourself when you were outside. Someone really should give you a bath. Or, maybe just put you out? Where is your widdle doggy door?"

She got up from her chair to walk towards us.

Please don't come over here. Please! I can't handle myself around you, dream girl.

Lizzie positioned herself between Paul and Maryanne and was standing right before me. She reached down to hold my hand. I immediately felt a surge of calming energy flow from her hand. Comforting, even. My heart was beating faster and slower, both at the same time. Our hands touched and I felt like

I had known her for a thousand years. Her touch was intense, and electrifying.

She looked deep in my eyes. "Well, aren't you a handsome devil? What's your name?" Her gorgeous smile was ringed with her soft, light pink lips. They looked more than welcoming and I wondered what it would be like to kiss her, to feel her lips pressed against mine as our tongues intertwined.

Rick! Snap out of it! Deal with what's in front of you.

"I'm Rick. Rick Blume," I stammered out as I stared at her stupidly.

"And what's your secret talent, handsome Rick?" she asked. I could still feel the deep connection from our hands. "You're running with a pretty mixed crew, so I assume you have some hidden talent? Something that might interest me?"

Talent? Fat chance. I'm a pathetic human being.

"Uhh…" I was frozen with nerves and couldn't speak.

Talk to her, dumbass! Say something!

I blurted out the first thing to come into my head: "I'm a Junior Sales Representative at Lightning Pop."

Yeah, that'll impress her. Soda boy.

"Oh, yes!" Her eyes twinkled. "Home to the great Carlos's Coke. I can't get enough of that stuff." I was dumbfounded that she knew anything about Lightning Pop.

Can vampires even drink soda?

"Well, Rick Blume, I'm Elizabeth Paynes. But you may call me Lizzie. And it is truly a pleasure to make your acquaintance." She released my hand back to me with a final, gentle squeeze. "And, as I'm sure you already know, I'm a vampire. Have been for quite some time now."

And how long is quite some time exactly? Should I be

asking her these questions? I'm not sure this is a conversation.

"One hundred and seventy-six years as a vampire, to be exact." She answered me without my asking.

How did she do that?! She can't read minds too, can she? I started sweating thinking that she might tap into my bottomless well of dirty thoughts about her. Some of the dirtiest.

Don't think about her ass. At least, not while she's here. Come on, Rick, let's keep it appropriate. Innocuous. Like cotton candy. Football games. Just don't look at any part of her body and you'll be fine.

Fuck, do I really need to get laid.

Lizzie moved even closer to me, gently pushing past Paul and Maryanne. "I could sense you watching me last night," she said softly. "No, it wasn't a dream, Rick. Everything you saw was actually happening in real-time. Did you enjoy the show?" She leaned in close and whispered directly in my ear, "Don't worry, it'll be our little secret." Her lips brushed my ear as she spoke, her breath warmed the side of my face, and I wanted her to keep touching me.

So, my dream was real. It wasn't a dream…? She really was doing those nasty things to Christo? Shit.

Paul had had it. Until she started whispering directly into my head, Paul had been very patient with Lizzie's invasion. But after she invaded his space, and then mine, he stepped up to her with a growl and broke the connection with her I was so thoroughly enjoying.

Thanks a lot, Paul.

"So, do you mind telling me why you're here? In my café drinking my coffee?" he asked with his voice raised. "You should be more careful of where you let yourself into.

Especially when you're trespassing on property owned by a werewolf. A werewolf, who has a Bogarden witch for a best friend."

Paul got in her face, but Lizzie was utterly unfazed.

"Oh, you're a Bogarden witch? I haven't come across one of your kind in at least a hundred years!" Lizzie said to Maryanne. "I thought your bloodline had died out. It's nice to know there's still at least one of you around. You're very, very powerful witches. Good people, too."

Maryanne smiled, and to my astonishment, ducked behind the counter to grab a muffin, then hand it to me.

"Well, thank you, Lizzie," Maryanne said as she pulled up one of the wooden chairs and took a seat next to Lizzie. "My great-grandmother went into hiding a few years before the Civil War after talk of a witch hunt across the north. She did her best to keep us away from all of it, and my family has been in hiding ever since. I am the last living Bogarden Witch, as far as I know."

"Well, I'm glad that there is at least one of you left," Lizzie said, patting the back of Maryanne's hand.

Paul was still glowering at Lizzie, but now with his hands in his pockets. "I'd still love to know why you let yourself into my café. I'm sorry to break up this little reunion we're all having here, but I want some damn answers. Now."

Yup, it's official; the werewolf is finally pissed off... I hope he doesn't go all Baskerville on everyone.

"Oh, pipe down Paul. I'm sure she has a good reason for coming here this morning. Isn't that right Lizzie?" Maryanne was defending her — she was sticking up for the vampire!

Maybe she came to see me? Pfft. Dream on, Rick.

"Well, yes. I am sorry, but I come bearing bad news. There

is a war brewing, and I'm afraid we're not going to be able to stop it... To stop him. I think we share a common enemy." Lizzie and Maryanne looked so natural and comfortable sitting next to each other at that tiny table it looked like they'd been friends forever.

"Who?" Paul shouted. He hadn't gotten a direct response as to why Lizzie broke into his café, and was impatient for some answers.

Lizzie sat quiet before lowering her eyes and whispering, "Mr Daggen."

Christo? Oh, shit. I definitely don't want him for an enemy. Especially if he's a vampire, on top of being terrifying.

I wondered what made Christo Lizzie's enemy.

Paul, seeming to read my mind, jumped in, "We've never had a problem with him here. Sure, he's a little shady and everyone knows he runs a hot poker game behind the dry-cleaners, but that's about it. I don't ask him questions, and he doesn't bother me. We stay out of each other's way." Paul sighed. "I really don't want any more problems — I have enough to deal with."

From the many years I had known Paul, I always thought of him as a gentle soul. I couldn't see him as a fighter. But he had a whole other side to him that I didn't know. The animal. But even with the wolf, I was pretty sure that he was still a gentle giant.

"He threatens to expose us. All of us," Lizzie said. Maryanne's eyes widened and she set her mug down, mid-sip. "He's out of control. He thinks he can kill whoever he wants without any consequences, and will wreak havoc on the entire city."

Expose what exactly? The Other World? I mean, she just

said that she was a vampire like it was nothing to hide.

"And what do you think he's going to expose? He only comes in here with Lazarus and his goons to buy coffee and muffins. Really." Paul walked to the counter and poured himself a cup of the coffee the sexy vampire had brewed before we arrived. "I don't have any issues with him here. I suppose I always suspected he might not be human, but I would have smelled him. The same way you could smell me," he said, looking intently at Lizzie.

"Christo and I are, as far as both of us know, two of the only three vampires in the city."

Paul took a swig of his coffee. "Three meaning you, Christo, and Lazarus, right?"

"Correct. We haven't turned anyone else, so it's just been the three of us. It can get kind of lonely after a while." I hated picturing the two of them together, and my stomach turned over in knots; I didn't want him to touch her, let alone fuck her.

Maryanne walked over to the counter and pulled out yet another chocolate chip muffin from the glass case and began to butter it with her knife. "I know what you mean," she said over her shoulder. "Thank God I have Paul. And now Rick, too." She flashed me a quick smile. "But being the only one of your kind can be extremely difficult. I wish I was part of a coven, but I don't know any other real witches."

She's actually my friend? I have a real friend... For the first time, I think.

Paul butted in, "Okay, okay. So there's you three vampires. Got it. But that doesn't explain how Christo threatens to expose us." He was getting impatient.

"By being careless. He's acting too rashly. He said he had

Lazarus kill Laura because she found out about us, somehow." Lizzie paused before saying, "I don't believe him."

I had almost forgotten about Dead Laura still stuffed in the back of Paul's car. *She's got to be getting warm by now. Boiling, even. I'll bet her eyeballs have turned to soup... Ugh. Gross.*

"Ever since he had Laura killed, Christo's been different. He just wants to hunt, kill, and fuck," Lizzie said soberly.

Fuck? Fuck.

The thought of them together continued to nauseate me.

"He's been unhinged lately. And violent." Lizzie looked down at her fingers, as if ashamed. "He... hurts me now."

If he lays one finger on her, so help me God. I will, I will, probably not do anything because Christo terrifies me...

There was an uncomfortable silence as we all absorbed what she was saying. "Do you want us to stop him from hurting you? Is that what this is about?" Paul asked in a caring tone. "I'm still trying to figure out why you broke into my place."

Lizzie slammed her fist onto the table, which shook the coffee mugs and sent a visible crack running through the tabletop. "He's a monster, and he needs to be stopped. You need to help me destroy him. Please." Lizzie's voice was strong and focused, but a single tear ran down her cheek. Paul grabbed a napkin and handed it to her.

"I'm sorry. I really am," Paul said. "I try to live a simple life: I don't want to bother anybody, and I don't want to be bothered by anybody. But I will help you," he looked at Maryanne. "We will help you kill Christo."

Maryanne had her arm around Lizzie's shoulder in a familiar, comforting way. She looked at Lizzie for a long time before saying, "Yes. It would be one less vampire in this world, which doesn't sound like such a terrible thing, does it?"

I had never killed anyone or anything before, except for mosquitoes and the odd cockroach. I was not a killer, but what Maryanne was saying made sense to me: kill the killer to stop the killing.

Paul summed up: "So you want our help to kill Christo. You want a witch and a werewolf to help a vampire kill another vampire. But not just any vampire — Christo Daggen, a man who's been coming into my café for as long as I can remember. Think about what you are asking me to do. Can you even prove to me that he is a vampire? I mean, you show up here a few times and now I'm just supposed to take your word as the truth and help you kill him? This whole thing is fucked up and ridiculous." Paul was pacing and furiously scratching his head. Lizzie walked over to the window.

"This is the only way I can feel the sun's warmth now. I'd give anything to be able to stand in its light again… I've forgotten what it feels like to be in the light." Lizzie spoke wistfully as she raised her hand to the window where the sun was shining through bright. "But yes. I can prove to you he is a vampire, if you want." Lizzie turned from the window to face Paul before saying, "He knows about you." She then looked to Maryanne, "He knows about both of you, and he will try to kill you."

"What exactly does he know?!" Paul shouted at her.

Maryanne walked over to Paul and set her hand on his shoulder before cooing, "Calm down. We don't need any accidents today."

Accidents? Like, a werewolf-sized accident? Yeah, calm down big guy.

Lizzie met Paul's gaze. "Christo knows there is a werewolf around here, and he assumes that it's someone close to Maryanne."

...Uh oh...

"And he knows that Maryanne is a witch, but I don't think he knows you are a Bogarden witch," Lizzie said to the pair, giving them little solace.

"What makes you think he doesn't know I'm Bogarden?" Maryanne asked.

"Because if he did, you'd be dead. I guarantee it. You are extremely dangerous to Christo. But also, by killing you, he would absorb the powers from your bloodline, making him almost indestructible. But he is already very strong." Paul and Maryanne looked at each other.

I had been burning with questions since Lizzie introduced herself, but didn't dare get in the middle of such tense negotiations. I decided to save my probing questions for later. Maybe a private interview with Lizzie.

Lizzie walked to the table and sat back down. She crossed her legs as she ran her fingers through her long blonde hair. "He's going to keep killing people if we don't stop him. And if he keeps killing people then humans will catch on, and they will hunt us down. Kill us. Each and every one of us."

Paul nodded his head in agreement. "The hunters would become the prey. The world order would collapse. Werewolves, vampires, witches and God-knows-what-else would go extinct." He looked out the window. "Gone forever."

Lizzie nodded solemnly. "And Christo would no longer be our only enemy; it would be us against the rest of the world."

'Us against the world'? That can't be good. I'm not sure

if I'm 'us' or 'world' at this point.

Maryanne licked her fingers clean of buttered chocolate-chip muffin crumbs before heading toward the doors of the café. She opened the blinds on two of the windows as she passed by them. "I'm going to go get Laura from the car," she said. "I'm sure she's getting warm sitting in a car with this crazy New York fall weather we've been having. Mother Nature is a fickle lady."

Lizzie poured herself another cup of coffee, but stopped halfway to ask, "You mean Laura, as in no longer alive, throat slit, murdered by Lazarus, boss lady Laura?"

Precisely. Now, Dead Laura.

Maryanne cracked a smile at Lizzie's question.

"That's the one!" she chirped. "I resurrected her the other night — It was a truly awesome sight to behold."

Yeah, watching her reanimate my dead boss was just peachy... These people seriously need to get some perspective. And some new hobbies. I should introduce them to poker.

"What are you going to do with her? I mean, she's still dead, right?" Lizzie asked.

Paul was elbow-deep changing the bags out of the cafe's small trash cans, but chimed in with, "Yeah, she's dead. I gotta say, Maryanne's getting really good at bringing dead things back to life." He slung a bag of trash over his shoulder. "And we're going to put her downstairs in the secret basement where I used to have to chain myself up. That was before I met Maryanne and before she helped me control the change." He walked out the back door to the alley and its mountains of full bags of trash.

Maryanne started to leave through the front door as she said, "What can I say? I like to think of myself as Jesus-in-training." The doors swung behind her as she headed to Paul's car.

That left us alone in the room. Though only for a brief moment, it was just her, and me. She looked at me and caught me already staring at her. It was painfully obvious that I was infatuated. I didn't know how to hide it.

Should I say something? I don't want to make it any more uncomfortable than it already is. Maybe it's more awkward if I don't say anything and just continue to stare at her?

I couldn't help it. Her golden yellow hair, her ocean-blue eyes, her gorgeous face and flawless body. Everything about her looked perfect. And I was dumbstruck; I had never spoken to a girl so gorgeous. Or any girl at length, really. Between my days as a soda jerk, and my nights as a drunken gambler, I wasn't exactly Casanova.

"Is there something on your mind?" she asked, breaking the awkward silence. "Or would you prefer to continue just staring at me?"

She noticed me staring? Smooth move, Rick. Just be cool, just be yourself.

"Umm… I'm okay just looking at you… I'm not really that great with words," I answered, trying to keep my cool.

"It's easy," she said. "Just tell me what's on your mind."

No, no, no, Rick. Definitely don't do that.

"I'm just trying to get used to all of this supernatural stuff," I said as off-handedly as I could, though hardly convincing.

"There's plenty to get used to!" Lizzie replied. "But if you want to know something about vampires, or other things from the Other World, let me know and I will tell you what I can." She stood up from the table and started to make her way to the door.

"Are you leaving?" I asked, desperation creeping into my voice.

"I'm going to go for a run and attempt to calm down. I'll be back, though; I hope your friends and I can figure out a way to eliminate Christo. For good." She swung the door open and looked back at me.

"It was lovely to meet you, Handsome Rick," she said, waving at me. "I do hope to see you again."

But it's daylight, and she's a vampire. Won't she burn up?!

"Hey, wait! What about the sun?" But she was gone before I could get the question out; one second, she was in front of me, foxy as anything, then in an instant she had completely disappeared. Almost like she was never there and my mind was playing tricks on me. I logically knew she was real and in front of me, but somehow time and space felt separate.

Paul returned through the back door, wiping his brow as he announced, "It's getting hot out there, Rick. Hey, where'd our new vampire *friend* go?"

I wish she was still here with me.

"I'm not entirely sure. She said she was going to go for a run and then try to figure out the Christo problem," I answered honestly.

"I bet you this whole ball of wax is going to get pretty freaking hairy." Paul winked at me as he laughed at his own joke.

"Yeah, Christo is probably going to be a pain in the ass." I tried to be as tough-guy as I could, but I knew Christo wouldn't go down without a fight. And because Christo had never lost at anything before, the fight would only end in death. His, or ours.

There was a knock on the door and I flinched and yelped, like a scared little kid. I turned to see Maryanne at the door holding onto Dead Laura's chains attempting to get her inside. Paul hurried over to help Maryanne get her through the door.

"Rick, a little help over here, please?" he demanded.

I stood in the doorway and grabbed onto the chains wrapped around the zombie's neck. With a gentle nudge we were able to get Dead Laura into the café. I didn't understand why Maryanne wasn't just giving her instructions like she normally did.

"Now, let's get her down to the basement," Maryanne said, huffing and puffing into the cafe.

"Yeah, give us just a sec. We'll get right to it," Paul said, Dead Laura's chains still in his giant hand.

We? Great. More undead physical labor.

I was stuck at Paul's Café with a witch and a werewolf, helping to take care of a zombie. The highlight of my morning had been a sexy vampire. I almost yearned for the boredom of Lightning Pop.

...Lizzie...

I hoped to see her again. Maybe even have an actual conversation with her. My need to see her again felt almost physical, though; I craved her, in so many ways.

Chapter Nine

The night was young but the alley was exceptionally dark. The skies were filled with thick, black clouds. A fat, grey rat scurried across the alley in search of its next meal. A couple walked hand in hand. The grumpy storm clouds were threatening rain, but otherwise the night was calm.

But an ancient vampire sat two stories above, perched on the rooftop without being seen or heard: Christo Daggen, one of the oldest vampires to walk the Earth. Daggen lurked above to watch the couple as they stumbled through the alley, waiting for the perfect moment for him to strike. The woman was giggling quietly as the man whispered in her ear. He reached down and gently slapped her ass through her cheap, red leather skirt.

"You like that, don't you?" the man whispered in his girlfriend's ear. She leaned into him and started to kiss his neck. "Hmmm. If you keep that up, you might have to take me right here in the alley." The woman gave him a playful push and he thudded against a steel dumpster, splashing pools of water beneath his feet.

"What're you waiting for?" she teased as she reached down and undid his pants with one hand. The man squeezed her chest firmly. The bottom of her shirt rose to reveal the soft skin of her lower abdomen and the base of her navel. She let out a small moan.

"Here I come, babe," he said into her ear before slamming his mouth against hers. It was violent and frantic, but the couple met each other with equal force.

The man and woman loudly smacked lips and licked each other's tongues. The woman thrust her hips against his undone jeans and started to slowly grind against his rapidly-stiffening cock, which was protruding from his shorts and his open fly. He moved his hands to the inside of her shirt and felt up her abdomen. Her stomach was flat, smooth, and long. He inched his fingers up to her breasts, and ran his fingertips along the fraying fabric along the underwire of her bra.

Christo was debating what to do with the amorous couple. He couldn't let them live — not after he'd taken the time to stalk them from two flights up. Plus, they were expendable. Wasting Christo's time, though? That would have been a real tragedy.

The ancient vampire could hear their hearts racing from his elevated perch. Faster and faster they beat as they caressed each other in the dark alley. The woman's head was tilted back, and Christo could see the skin from her bare neck gleaming through the shadows. It looked soft and welcoming. He licked his lips in anticipation of sinking his fangs into her naked, pulsing throat. Christo was starving, and could tell the alley girl was going to be absolutely delectable — trashy people always were.

He jumped from the edge of the roof to the alley below and landed directly on the dumpster behind the couple without making a sound. The humans were so engrossed with each other they didn't notice the sudden appearance of the blood-sucking creature now looming over them.

Christo reached down and swiftly grabbed the man's

throat with one hand and started to squeeze. The man coughed and sputtered as Christo drained him of his lifeforce. The woman screamed at the top of her lungs and tried to run, but Christo grabbed the back of her neck and turned her around so she was forced to face him. He looked at her face and held her gaze, confronting her with his bright red eyes and overly-dilated pupils.

"You are going to stay calm. When I release you, you will stand still and you won't make a sound." Christo stared at the woman as he commanded her.

"I won't make a sound," she repeated flatly. Christo released her and turned to the man but the woman remained completely still, as if hypnotized.

"You won't make a sound, either," Christo hissed at the man. "And you will not move when I release you." Christo's words echoed around the now pitch-black alley as he let go of the man's throat. The man stood still and obeyed Christo's commands, like he was his pet. "I won't move," he said.

Christo stood for a moment and looked at the couple. He was thinking about what he wanted to do next. He could snap their necks and drink them dry and then vanish without leaving any trace of himself, but that was not good enough. It wasn't brutal enough for Christo; he enjoyed inflicting pain upon his victims because it brought him pleasure. He wanted to torture them so badly that they would try to cry out and beg for mercy, though they'd be unable while under his power. It was all part of his game: he liked the hunt, but he lived for the kill. It was the only thing that gave him any pleasure apart from sex.

"Are you going to kill us?" the woman asked Christo, casually wondering if she was going to die.

"Yes," Christo answered immediately as he ran his fingers

through her hair. He suddenly yanked a handful of hair from her head and put it to his nose and inhaled her scent deeply. "But don't worry, my dear. I'm not going to kill you right away," he said. He dropped her hair on the ground and stomped it as if it were a bug. He turned to the man, who looked frightened. The woman looked frightened, too, but neither could move while under Christo's sway. He was pleased to see that the couple was terrified.

Christo laughed a little bit to himself before he announced, "I'm going to make you watch me fuck your girlfriend. Then I'm going to make her watch me kill you. Once you're out of the way I'm going to sink my fangs into that beautiful neck of hers. She will die slowly, and in pain. But on the bright side, I will be satisfied for a little while… Hopefully."

The man's eyes opened wider as Christo monologued, fully grasping what awaited. The woman's eyeliner ran down her cheek as tears pooled in her eyes. Christo moved close and leaned in to give the woman a malicious kiss. He purposefully pierced her soft mouth with his front fang, which popped it open like a small balloon and blood poured from her trembling lower lip. The man watched as the blood dripped from his girlfriend's mouth and ran down her chin.

Christo loved the taste of fresh blood — nothing made him more aroused than drinking blood from a human like a wine from a glass. Humans were necessary, but disposable; after these two he would simply find some other innocent people to drink. Even when not draining them Christo liked to exercise control over humans — he was a god amongst men, and had been for over a thousand years. And he would not let anything threaten his position. He was brutal and arrogant because he knew humans were powerless against him.

"Take off your shirt," Christo ordered the woman. She immediately undressed so she was standing in the alley in her skirt, knee high socks, and her bra.

"It looks like you two have some things you need to work on. Your girlfriend is going to strip for anyone who asks? I can see where that could create some trust issues." Christo laughed at the man. "But get a load of this—" Christo grabbed at the woman's chest and harshly squeezed her flesh. "Very nice. Now take off your skirt."

She reached behind herself and pulled down the zipper on the back of her skirt then stepped out of the cheap fabric, leaving her in just her bra, panties and socks. The man watched as his girlfriend became Christo's powerless puppet.

"She is an angel, isn't she? Just look at that body. You're a lucky man. Or should I say, you were." Christo stepped behind the woman and pressed his pelvis against the cheeks of her ass, feeling excited. "This is going to be fun…" he said devilishly.

"Bend over," Christo ordered. He pushed on her shoulder blades to force her to bend forward. "Pull down your underwear."

The woman dropped her panties to her ankles and revealed her sex to Christo. Her slit was bald, beautiful, and perfectly pink. Christo unsnapped the front of his pants and pulled out his bulging organ. He walked over to the man, grabbed him by the side of his head and forced his head forward as Christo smacked his face with his massive dick.

"Are you ready for me to fuck your girlfriend, you pathetic waste of life?" The man still couldn't move. He couldn't speak, and remained frozen in Christo's thrall as his girlfriend was assaulted.

Christo moved behind the woman and let out a low, mean moan. He then rammed his cock deep inside her. She winced but was unable to move, speak, or resist. Christo continued to pound her from the back, over and over again. He forced himself in deeper with every thrust. Faster and faster he rammed her, now using his vampire speed to fuck. Christo wanted every thrust to hurt her; the more pain she was in just meant more pleasure for him.

The woman's face was covered in tears and running makeup but she couldn't force Christo off her. She wanted to scream out in pain, which Christo could sense, so he fucked her even harder. He roared, stiffened, and then shuddered as he finally filled up her tight slit with a load of his vampiric self and shouted towards the heavens during his release. Christo pulled his shaft out from inside the woman and it was covered in blood. He ran his fingers along his bloody cock, then put his fingers in his mouth and sucked the woman's blood from them.

"Nothing beats fresh blood," he said as he turned his attention to the man still frozen in fear. "Now it's your turn to have some fun."

Christo grabbed the man by his throat and lifted him off the ground. The man was powerless; Christo was too strong. The man was choking and spitting and his face was turning blue as Christo allowed him just enough oxygen to survive.

"Have you had enough?" Christo asked the paralyzed man. "Are you ready to die?"

The man's only response was the rasping sounds of him gasping for air. Christo squeezed his throat and felt the man's trachea collapse under his grip.

"Ugh, let's get this over with." Christo opened his mouth

wide to reveal to the man the set of razor-sharp fangs that were about to end his mortal life. The man stared at the deadly fangs with his bulging eyes and sucked at the air in an attempt to call for help with his crushed vocal cords, but no sound came.

Christo forced the man's head back as he continued to carefully choke him. He knew that the small amount of pressure the base of the skull puts on the spinal cord when a human's head is tipped back is enough to exponentially increase the amount of pain experienced. And Christo had no qualms with causing more pain; it had become his raison d'être.

Christo slowly and carefully sunk his fangs into the man's neck. The tip punctured each layer of skin before tapping into the man's carotid artery.

He could feel the hot, thick blood flow into him through his fangs, giving him an immediate infusion of energy. And the rush of oxygen and hemoglobin through Christo's desiccated veins left him feeling euphoric; a high better than any synthetic drug, and more powerful than his orgasm.

He saw flashes of the man's life as he drank — key moments that defined his mortal life. Christo watched as he graduated from high school. And when he got his first job as a waiter at a local pizza shop. And when he first met his girlfriend on the subway — the same girl now lying motionless, covered in her own blood.

Christo's visions stopped when there was no blood left to drink. The man was empty, dried up and dead. Christo extracted his fangs from the man's neck and dropped him to the ground like he was a rag doll. The body hit the pavement with a dull thud as the corpse's face landed in a puddle, splashing water on the woman's feet, soaking her socks. The man's lifeless eyes were wide open, staring at nothing. Raindrops rinsed the blood from the man's neck, revealing two tiny punctures: the vampire's calling card.

Christo stood tall and breathed in deep. He felt invigorated. He was calm, euphoric, and emboldened. He saw no reason to give a damn about anything other than his own unstoppable needs as he let the high from the man's blood rush to his head. Like any user, Christo wanted the feeling to last forever, but knew that it wouldn't. He turned his attention back to the woman, who was still hypnotized and standing almost totally naked in front of her dead boyfriend.

"Well, your boyfriend tasted good, but I'll bet you're gonna taste even better, little lady." He brushed the woman's hair from the side of her neck. "You know, I'm awfully tempted just to turn you and make you my bride until the end of eternity. I would love to fuck you again. But then I would have to teach you how to be a vampire — all the dos and the don'ts. Hah! Who am I kidding? There aren't any DON'Ts. Gah, except for the sun. Either way, it's a lot of work that I don't want to deal with, so I'll just kill you. It's nothing personal. And I won't torture you too much. I promise."

Christo stood before the woman and was struck by her physical beauty. He again ran his fingers across her neck, and then pushed her bra strap off her shoulder.

"Take off your bra," he ordered.

The woman removed her bra swiftly exposing her small perfectly rounded nipples. He watched the rain fall on her and drip down her body. Christo pinched her nipples harshly, and she wanted to run but she still couldn't move. He slid one of his long fingernails down her stomach and scratched her deep beneath her skin. He left a trail of blood running to her groin, and he imagined of her body erupting with blood like a volcano. He sliced to her sex with his nails and she remained powerless, naked and afraid. Christo forcefully shoved two fingers up inside her and again she wanted to pull away.

In and out, over and over. He shoved his fingers into her, nails extended. Further and further he went up inside her until there was nowhere else for him to go. Christo could see her heartbeat throbbing in her jugular and could tell she was in excruciating pain. The color was draining from the woman's skin and he could tell she was on the verge of death. Christo quickly thrust his fangs firmly into the side of her throat and instantly felt the warmth of her blood rushing through him. He drank deeply, swallowing every drop greedily. Just as he'd suspected, she was sweet and delectable. The woman's eyes quickly rolled back as Christo swiftly pulled his fingers from her insides, ripping a steaming pile of guts from her belly. He kept drinking.

There was a loud crash of thunder at the same moment the blood stopped flowing from the limp body. The woman was dead and emptied out. Christo withdrew his fangs and let the lifeless, naked corpse fall to the ground. With a thud, the body landed next to the other and Christo smiled, pleased with the carnage.

"You were awfully tasty." Christo licked his lips. "What a shame you had to die," he said as he looked at the two dead bodies before him.

Christo positioned the bodies so they were holding hands, the woman's right arm crossed over her chest below her breasts, her head resting on her dead boyfriend's shoulder.

Christo stood tall and stretched his arms, coaxing the blood infusion to flow the full length of his ancient body.

"What a mess," he said, looking around for a way to cover up his frenzy. There was a large plastic sheet in the dumpster behind him which he used to cover the bodies, taking one final mental snapshot as he did. Christo wanted to remember them; he was thankful for the blood he had extracted. The dirty plastic sheet covered the expired bodies — only the toes of their shoes were visible, peeking out from the edge.

Christo's superhuman ears picked up a barely-perceptible noise, and he guessed he was no longer alone. A large crow took flight from down the alley and hovered above him for a moment.

"Who's there?!" Christo shouted, staring at the crow. He stood for a moment before putting his pants back on. "I asked WHO'S THERE," he shouted. "Show yourself. Don't make me mad, asshole."

He heard faint footsteps on the rooftops above him but all he could see were the raindrops ricocheting off slick surfaces. He spun around, and in that instant, Lizzie appeared before him. She stood with her arms crossed, frowning.

"Well, well, well. Somebody's certainly getting better at sneaking," he said to her with a smile.

"You know what they say: practice makes perfect." She looked at the two sets of toes beneath the plastic on the ground behind Christo. "What the hell, Christo? What did you do?" she asked, though the question was more-or-less rhetorical.

"Oh, nothing major. Just two bloodbags who thought they'd try to steal my wallet," Christo answered with a wry smile. "They must have been hard up for cash. It's hard to make a living nowadays. Desperate times call for desperate measures." His mock compassion made it clear he had no remorse.

"Really? You seriously expect me to believe that? You don't even carry a wallet."

Christo turned to the dead bodies. "What do you want me to say? I was hungry and horny, and they were in the wrong place at the wrong fucking time."

Lizzie appeared before him in an instant and slapped his face with all of her vampire strength.

"Stop that," he said. "Everyone has needs." She swung at him again but he ducked her fist. The one slap she gave him was one more than anyone ever had, and he wasn't going to let her make a habit of it.

"Must you keep killing random humans for pleasure? I thought you liked it here, enjoyed this city, Christo. Do you want to be forced to leave?" Lizzie pleaded. She knelt before the bodies to inspect them.

"Forced to leave?" Christo snapped. "How would I be forced to go anywhere I don't want? I am the fastest, strongest immortal. Who's going to challenge me? You?! Hah! You might be immortal, but I am practically invincible. Nothing can harm me." He sneered at her before warning, "I suggest you remember that if you are going to continue speaking to me in that tone of voice."

Lizzie pulled the plastic tarp back to reveal the victims' faces. "But what exactly do you think is going to happen if humans find out about us? Do you really think they'll welcome vampires with open arms? No! They will kill us, or study us, because they're afraid of the unknown." Lizzie replaced the tarp, not wanting to look at the mangled bodies any longer. "You should bury them." Unlike Christo, she felt sorry for the couple. "They deserve that, at least, Christo."

Christo pulled a cigarette from his pocket and attempted

to light it with a flick of his Zippo. It took three tries to get the spark to ignite because of the rain. "Humans are only good for food and pleasure, so I'm not gonna waste my time burying them. Fuck 'em." Lizzie ripped the cigarette from his mouth and threw it to the ground.

"They are people, Christo! They have jobs, families, and friends who care about them — people who will notice and give a shit if they go missing. But I bet you didn't think about any of that," Lizzie scolded. She wanted him to understand the severity of the situation. "What will you do if they figure out you're the one killing random people? Humans have a term for that: serial killer."

Christo was unfazed. His blasé attitude made it clear he didn't care about anyone or anything besides himself and his dick. "I guess I'd better make sure nothing points back to me, then," he hissed.

Christo tore the tarp off the bodies. He extended his pointer finger and his nail grew even longer, and then dug into the woman's abdomen, right below her navel. He carved ELIZABETH one letter at a time, using the slice he'd already made in her belly as the 'I'.

"There you go, now nobody'll ever know I had anything to do with this," Christo said, smiling at Lizzie.

"What the fuck?! Are you threatening me because I want you to stop killing innocent humans? Trust me: Eventually they will figure this out. Somebody will *find* us out. And then, they'll come for us. All of us." Lizzie spoke clearly and loudly to further impress upon Christo just how reckless his actions were.

Christo stepped back from Lizzie and the bodies and began to fade into the night. "Let them come," he said while laughing out loud. "I'll kill each and every one of 'em." And, with a final chuckle, Christo vanished.

Lizzie was alone in the alley with only the bodies bearing her name for company. She dolefully heaved the bodies from the ground and into the dumpster, then threw the tarp in to cover them up. "I'm sorry," she whispered as she shut the lid of the dumpster tight. It wasn't the first time she was left to clean up after Christo, but she hoped it would be the last.

Chapter Ten

I sat at the lone chair in what passed for a kitchen in my apartment, and listened to the rain pound the ground and windowpanes. The empty gin bottles and beer cans were piled up in the corner of my makeshift kitchen, flowing over and out of the box I used for returnables. Rivers of small raindrops gushed down the glass of the lone window so I could barely make out the apartment complex next door.

The kitchen was small and sparsely outfitted: my wooden chair, the refrigerator, the microwave, and the folding card table I'd bought for under twenty dollars that served as my kitchen table. The grey and white tiled floor was cracked and plastered with light brown stains from me spilling coffee while I was drunk or hungover. A single poster of the American flag hung on the wall next to the fridge. It was the closest thing I had to decorations in my apartment — I wasn't exactly domestic.

I reached across the table and grabbed the only thing on it — a newspaper from three days ago I'd bought on a whim.

Let's see what passed for front page news this week.

I put on my glasses to make out the headline.

Damn, my eyesight is getting terrible. Wait, is that Laura on the front page?

I looked down — now able to see what I was reading — at a large picture of my dead boss, Laura Spilkotton. She looked good. Happy. Better than she ever had while I knew her.

Ugh, know her, I guess. Though dead and rotting and flesh-eating are probably better descriptors for her these days.

The picture must have been from before she started working for Lightning Pop, because she was never happy there. Not for as long as I was there, anyways. I chuckled remembering when one of the temps brought her a birthday cake that she then shoved in his face while yelling at him. I had assumed that was her way of saying thank you.

Under the bullshit photo was the headline, LOCAL WOMAN MURDERED. The article reported she was murdered at her workplace and there were no leads, but there were two witnesses.

Witnesses?

I figured this was most likely a reference to Tony and myself, but we weren't witnesses. We hadn't witnessed a damn thing; I found her dead in her office chair, and Tony called 911. That was it.

I put the paper down with an aggrieved sigh and got up to fill my mug with more coffee. I'd been subsisting on caffeine for weeks and felt the need for something with more of a kick. Food. I didn't know how to cook and wasn't about to learn, so I made peace with relying on Paul and Maryanne for all my meals. I had gotten used to my cupboards being bare.

In the meantime, more coffee. Well, coffee and liquor. But since all my gin bottles had been emptied at the parties I'd been hosting for me, myself, and I, coffee would have to do.

Looking towards the coffee pot sitting on my naked countertop, I noticed the light on my answering machine blinking red with a number one on the display.

Someone called? Me? That doesn't happen too often. Not unless it's work. And they usually call my cell.

Work. With Laura gone I had no idea of what to expect. I pushed play to listen to what the machine had to tell me and a deep voice rose from its guts, speaking to me from behind the red blinking light.

"Hello, Mr Blume. This is Detective Jackson Lee with the NYPD. We met last week at your work. I got a chance to look over the security footage, and so far, there's nothing suspicious from that day. Unfortunately, Ms Spilkotton's body was disturbed in a cemetery recently and I wonder if maybe you heard something about that. If you know any details about that, or anything, please give me a call at your earliest convenience. I'll also be speaking with your coworker, ehh — what's his name… — Tony, at some point. The NYPD thanks you in advance for your cooperation." <beep>

The deep voice ceased, and I was left wondering why Detective Lee would think I knew anything about Laura being dug up. While I did absolutely know who did it, how could he know that? Did he know I was at the cemetery?

That's not good — he must think I had something to do with her murder… Has he been following me? Does he consider me an actual suspect? I didn't have any type of record or any problems with the police, and I hoped to keep it that way.

I was still thinking about the disconcerting phone message when I heard a tap-tap-tap at my kitchen window. I looked but couldn't see through the pouring rain, so shrugged it off and returned to my coffee. I attempted to fill up my cup without adding more stains to the tiles when there was another tap on my window, much louder than the first. I was more confused than scared, given the only thing outside my fourth-floor apartment was the rickety fire-escape, which I didn't trust to support the weight of anything larger than a fat pigeon.

I spun around to catch sight of whatever was making the noise, fully expecting to see a bird or something trying to escape from the storm. But instead saw that Lizzie — gorgeous Lizzie — was squatting on the fire escape, tapping on my window. I was so surprised I dropped the coffee pot and hurried to the window as the pot shattered beneath my feet, leaving bits of glass scattered across the kitchen floor.

"Oh, my god!" I yelled as I reached the sill.

She was wearing blue jeans with a red, collared shirt. The top two buttons were open and her throat and cleavage looked inviting. Her clothes were drenched, and so was her hair. I'd only seen her a few times before, but still I thought she looked more beautiful than ever. There was something very appealing about seeing her soaking wet. I'd wanted her since the first time I'd seen her, but today my attraction to her was different, more intense. Maybe it was seeing her so damn wet. Or maybe it was the thrill of her coming to my window to escape the storm. All of her clothes were drenched from the pouring rain.

I tried to quickly unlock and raise the lower pane of the window, but had to jostle the wood to get it to budge. Lizzie smiled from her perch as she watched me struggle, and it made me want to help her. To save her, no matter the cost. A chance to see her smile was worth risking everything.

With the window finally open I leaned out into the rain and asked, "Are you all right?"

"I've been better," she said quietly. I could barely hear her over the rain.

Wow. She looks amazing in the rain.

I saw her for just a second before the rain steamed over my lenses. "Why don't you get out of the rain?" I asked, extending my hand. She stared at me blankly then said, "You have to invite me in — it's a vampire thing. I can't come in unless I'm invited, Rick." She paused for a moment as the raindrops pinged off the fire escape. "You should know that once you invite me in, I can enter whenever I'd like. Whether you want me to come in or not."

So that's a real thing? She could literally come in and kill me in my sleep — am I really okay with this?

I hesitated. My most fundamental human instincts were telling me not to invite a vampire into my home. At no point had she hinted towards wanting to harm me, but I was trying to apply logic to the situation, however absurd.

"Please come in, Lizzie," I said, even as I continued to wonder how to do the right thing. Inviting a vampire into my home probably wasn't the smartest thing I had ever done, but for some reason I wasn't afraid of her; I figured if she wanted me dead that would be the end of it. She'd asked for help to take Christo down, which I took as a sign she was going to let me keep breathing.

She took my hand as I helped her climb through my window. I tried not to stare at her ass as she clambered into my kitchen, but failed miserably. Her jeans were stuck to her skin and I wondered if she was wearing panties as her soaking shirt clung to the curves of her body. I could see the faint outline of her nipples standing erect, and a piercing in her navel through her wet shirt. I craved her.

God, I would give anything to be with her for a night.

"Watch your step," I said. "I wasn't expecting to see someone sitting outside my window, so I dropped the coffee pot. Look out — there are pieces of glass everywhere. I'm really sorry."

She stepped in, released my hand, and looked at the broken glass on my floor. "So, I frightened you?" she asked coyly.

How do I answer that without seeming like a total coward?

All I could do was look at her.

"It's all right," she said. "I'm used to scaring people. Do you have a broom and a dustpan?" she asked looking around. "I guess since I'm the one who scared you this is really my fault."

I pulled the broom from next to the fridge and said, "You don't have to do this — I'll take care of it after you leave." I think she and I both knew that I was lying.

"It's really no problem. And who said anything about me leaving?" Lizzie said with a flirtatious smile. In one swift, fluid motion she took the broom from my hands, pulled out the dustpan, swept up the glass, and returned the broom and dustpan to my hands. Every bit of glass that had been on my floor a few seconds earlier was now cradled in the dustpan in my hands. "Now you don't have to take care of it later." She walked to the kitchen sink and wrung out her wet hair, a splash of rain landing loudly in the sink.

"Holy shit. That was impressive. You... You did all that before I could even blink," I marveled. I turned to dump the glass into the already overflowing garbage. "Do you ever get tired of being superhuman?" I knew I shouldn't be prying into a vampire's business but my mortal curiosity got the better of me. "Because, honestly, I don't think I'd ever get tired of having your powers. Your abilities... They amaze me... *You* amaze me."

Don't get weird, stupid.

Lizzie grinned. Her cheeks were turning a shade of light pink. "No, it doesn't get old. I really enjoy being a vampire, most of the time." She paused and sighed deeply before continuing, "That's why I'm so concerned about Christo. He could seriously screw up my life here. I spent a lot of years learning how to control myself, while learning who I really am. So now that I'm actually happy — here, in New York — I can't let anyone put that at risk. Not even Christo."

The mere mention of Christo's name summoned mental images of them together, of her fucking him. My hatred for him was reaching new heights and fairly irrational; I wanted to kill Christo because he'd had sex with Lizzie, and I hadn't. Jealousy was my only motivator. Sure, he was a threat to humans, but that's not why I wanted him dead.

That bastard — he'd better not touch her again.

I tried to stop thinking about the two of them together but I couldn't get the images out of my head. Her on top of him, him inside of her. I was getting angrier by the second as my macho jealousy raged.

"So, what are you doing here?" I asked, shaking my head in confusion. "Is there something I can help you with, or something you need?"

Oh, and how the hell do you know where I live?

I didn't want to push her away, but I did want some answers; I couldn't figure out why she would show up at my window.

Lizzie sat in my one and only kitchen chair and sighed before saying, "I'm here because of Christo. I had nowhere else to go."

Of course, more Christo…

"What about Christo? I used to go to his poker games quite a bit, but I don't really know him, or talk to him. Honestly, I don't think he likes me much."

She sat quietly and stared as I blathered, completely cutting her off. I quickly realized I needed to just shut up.

"Look, I know you don't have much to do with him, Rick, but Christo's doing a lot of things he shouldn't be doing. He's drawing way too much attention and eventually — or, soon! — he's going to create some serious problems for your friends. And me."

Having Laura murdered wasn't enough?

"What do you mean? What's he doing?" She was obviously tense, and had gotten visibly anxious after mentioning him. I could tell she was afraid of him, or at least afraid of what he might do.

"He killed two more innocent people tonight. He's, like, unhinged. I didn't know what to do. You were the first person I thought of… I don't know why, because you're human — I can't expect you to get into it with Christo. He'd kill you before you even saw him coming."

Why would he kill me? Granted, I wanted to kill him, but I hadn't given him any explicit reason to come after me. Still, I knew she was right: there was no way I could fight Christo Daggen.

"He killed two people, and then you came here? What if he followed you — I don't want him to come after me. What if he comes after me? How am I supposed to stop him?" A beautiful vampire was dripping wet in my kitchen after seeing two people murdered and I was whining. I'd graduated from jealousy, to cowardice, and I wanted her to reassure me.

There's no way I could stop him. If he wants me dead, I'm dead.

"Rick, calm down," she said firmly, sounding rational. "He didn't follow me. He had no reason to, and I'm pretty sure he trusts me... But he killed them in an alley behind Paul's. I watched him, and then confronted him about it."

He killed two people and she just watched? I didn't think she'd helped him kill them, but I was in a state.

"Why didn't you try to stop him?" I asked.

"You don't understand, there was nothing I could do. He is older than me, and so much stronger. If I'd tried to stop him I'd be lying dead in that alley, too. Right alongside that couple. He's got to be one of the first vampires... I've never seen such power."

Would Christo actually kill Lizzie? I knew I wouldn't be able to stop him, but Christo was clearly a menace.

"You said you confronted him — what did you say? I mean, he can't just go around killing random people, right? Did you call the police?"

Lizzie looked down at her lap. I was scolding her, like an ass. My only excuse was that I was terrified and had no idea of how to appropriately respond to all this vampire drama.

This is not good. This is really not good.

"I'm not an idiot, Rick. He doesn't give a damn about what I say or think," she said. I could hear the conviction in her voice. She really didn't think Christo could be stopped. "In the end, Christo Daggen is going to do whatever the fuck he wants because he thinks he's invincible. And, honestly, I don't know what *will* bring him down, so maybe he's right."

Through force of habit, or addiction, I walked to the fridge to look for a drink, but the fridge was still empty. "Don't vampires just casually kill people?" I was grasping for something, anything to latch onto to bring me back to Earth. "Like isn't that what they do?" I was trying my best to understand.

The thought of her killing someone didn't sit well with me. I couldn't see her doing that to someone, and yet couldn't stop imagining her ripping someone's throat to pieces to suck his blood. I didn't want to believe she was a monster like Christo.

"Yes, we have to have blood to survive. But there's no rule that it has to be human. Most of the time I feed off of small animals. But when I do kill a human it's either self-defense, or someone who actually deserves it. The last guy was a piece of work, beating his wife and kids and other bullshit. He was delicious, and I really enjoyed killing him."

Yup, it sounds like he deserved it.

"What... What exactly did you do to him?" I managed to ask out of morbid curiosity. It was a wholly inappropriate question.

She locked eyes with me before purring, "I gave him the best blow job of his life and then I bit his neck. I drank as much of his blood as I could then I ripped off his head and tore his body apart. I made it look like he was the victim of a lunatic serial killer. I usually just burn the bodies, but he deserved a special treatment."

I had no idea she could be so violent. It didn't change the way I thought about her, but did confirm that I barely knew her.

"Wow. Okay. That's graphic, but — it sounds like he probably deserved what he got." I decided to pull my container of instant coffee from the cupboard since my coffee pot had recently been smashed. I put a cup of water in the microwave to boil. "So, do you want to go to the police? You can prove to them you are a vampire, and then maybe they could come up with a plan for dealing with Christo?" I heard how ridiculous this was as I said it out loud, but I didn't have any other decent ideas.

Lizzie turned her head to stare out the rain-battered window as I was making the inane suggestion. She was still sitting at my small kitchen table. "He is trying to pin the murders on me," she said quietly.

"How?" I asked. I was concerned, and concerned for her. "Can he do that?" I asked again.

She was silent for a moment before replying, "He carved my name into the girl's stomach. He spelled out ELIZABETH. It might take the police a little while to figure it out, but eventually, Christo is going to blow our cover. He doesn't care. He said he'd kill anyone who gets in his way."

Anyone. Uh oh — I'm anyone! Can he really not be stopped?

The thought of an immortal god battling against the world was beginning to truly unnerve me. How would humans cope with an adversary with strength and speed that outstripped the strongest of men? Maybe the best idea was to try to keep him docile, to please him?

"What did Christo do with the bodies?" I asked, worried what she was going to say. "Did... Did he eat them?" I knew I sounded like an idiot.

"No, he didn't *eat* them. I took care of them the best I could. I wanted to bury them but Christo wouldn't let me. I wrapped them in a sheet of plastic, and they're in one of the dumpsters in the alley behind Paul's." She was open and honest and I still wasn't sure why she trusted me. I hadn't proven myself to her, so she must have felt the same connection I did the first time we touched.

"You did what you thought was best." I wanted to make her feel better but didn't know how. I'd never had a close call with a dead body before Laura, and now I had to consider two more in the alley behind Paul's. Christo needed to be stopped.

"I'm really sorry I showed up unannounced and just dumped all of this on you, Rick. I just didn't know where else to go. I guess I just thought that you might understand. You know, with what happened to Laura."

I held her hand in mine and realized how glad I was that she showed up at my window.

"You never have to apologize for coming to see me." I was trying to reassure her, and be romantic. Suddenly, she picked up my hand and put it to her mouth. Lizzie opened her lips and lightly kissed the pads of my fingertips. It was innocent and intimate and sent my mind reeling. I'd never been kissed like that — by anyone. Instinctively I pulled away. I was horny, and a basket case of emotions, and in a scenario not of my making.

What the hell do I do now?

"Are you going to go home tonight?" I asked. My hands wouldn't stop shaking and I was trembling with fear and excitement, and I prayed she didn't notice my nervous tics.

"I don't have a home," she replied. "But I'll be fine."

I wondered how someone like her — an ageless, supernatural being — couldn't have a home. I wasn't about to ask her why, though. When she wanted to tell me about her past, she would. In her own time.

"You're welcome to stay in my bed tonight," I said

without realizing how it sounded. "Uh, I can sleep in my recliner."

That's where I usually end up, anyways, too drunk and lazy to make it to the bed.

"That's sweet, Rick, but I don't want to be an imposition."

Imposition? My god, you'd be the first girl in my bed. Ever. I really wanted her to stay the night.

"Really?" she asked me.

"Please. It's really no problem." I insisted that she stay while avoiding the fact that she responded to a question I'd only asked in my mind.

"All right. If you insist." She relented.

I couldn't believe that a girl was going to spend the night in my apartment — the first in all my thirty-six years. And not just any girl — this girl. Lizzie. Perhaps the most beautiful girl I had ever seen. What should I do? What should I say? I had almost no experience with this kind of thing. Girls. Women. Zero experience.

"You're welcome to stay as long as you like. I'm not sure I have anything good to eat, but I could run to the store if you want something." I then remembered the pounding rain and hoped she wouldn't want a snack.

"Don't worry," she giggled. "If I get hungry, I'll just eat you." Lizzie pointed at me and smiled.

Fuck. I hope she's kidding.

"Ha-ha. You're not serious, though. Right?" I asked, feeling stupid.

"No, Rick. I'm not going to have you for dinner tonight. I had a squirrel and a stray cat on the way here. Fingers crossed I didn't catch rabies or anything dangerous," she laughed.

That's all I need: rabies. And shit — I should change the

sheets before she goes to lay down. They've got to be six weeks old. At least.

"Can I borrow one of your shirts to sleep in?" Lizzie asked. "My clothes are still soaked." She pulled her shirt away from her body, accidentally revealing her smooth stomach. I tried not to stare, but I was mesmerized by her body. I could see that her side was tattooed with bright forms and colors that wrapped around her navel.

Holy shit, everything about her is perfect.

"Umm..." I stammered, still staring at her body, "I can grab you a shirt from my bedroom. Just give me a second." I hurried across the apartment to the bedroom, through sexual tension so palpable and so thick it could be cut with a knife. Or the erection piercing from my shorts. I couldn't get her body out of my head — I wanted her more than anything. There was more to her than her body, which was driving me wild, and I was set on learning everything about her. I craved her.

I can't believe this is happening. This has got to be a dream.

I pulled a t-shirt from my dresser and rushed back out to the kitchen to give it to her. "This is clean," I said as I tossed it to her.

"Great — thanks. Worst case scenario I just sleep naked, right?"

Please sleep naked. Please. I've never seen a girl naked in person before. But my God, you don't need to know that.

"Do you have a place where I can change?" she asked. She flashed her gorgeous smile, which made my stomach flip-flop and my toes tingle. I didn't think I could be even more drawn to her, but somehow, in that moment, I was.

"The bathroom's over there," I said, gesturing to the door. "I'll change the sheets while you're *ahem* getting changed."

Because I never change my fucking sheets.

Just as I started towards the musty sheets, Lizzie vanished and I heard sounds from the bathroom where she was getting changed.

God damn, she is fast. Really fast.

I stripped the sheets from my bed and turned to throw them on the floor when I saw Lizzie standing in the bedroom doorway. She was leaning against the wall wearing my long t-shirt. It stopped halfway down her thighs. She had put her blonde hair up in a ponytail and it hung over the front of her right shoulder.

Oh christ, I gave her a fuck-me shirt.

"I'd say it fits, Rick. Wouldn't you?" She did a little twirl. I felt like panting, or drooling, or howling but instead stood still and, unsure of what to say, I nodded my head in agreement.

Say something. Anything.

After about ten seconds of silence, I was able to mutter, "It looks really good."

It looks really good? C'mon, Rick.

"Thanks," she answered.

Lizzie walked over to my bed, and in the blink of an eye the clean sheets were on, and the bed was made. Fresh, clean, and waiting.

I'm never going to get used to her speed.

"You looked like you were struggling so I thought I would just help you a little," Lizzie said as she took a seat on the edge of my bed. She tapped the bed next to her and motioned me to take a seat beside her. I stood still for a minute and wondered what I should do. She continued to motion for me to sit next to her and all I could do was stare.

"Come, sit, Rick. I promise I won't bite."

What if you change your mind?

"I won't. Not unless you ask me to," Lizzie said, before I could even finish my thought.

"Are you reading my mind?" I asked, looking for confirmation.

"I guess I am, but normally, I don't. But with you it's different from other humans. I'm different. I don't know why, but it's one of the reasons I'm drawn to you."

You're drawn to me?

"You're drawn to me? Really?" I couldn't believe what was happening.

Lizzie took my hand and placed it on her lap, slowly sliding it up her thigh. "Why is that so hard for you to believe?"

If I'm honest with her she might leave. I don't want her to know how lame I am.

"Well…" I stopped for a second. I was nervous and didn't know how to get the words out. "You see, nobody's ever been drawn to me before. There's never been a girl interested in me." I sighed deeply.

"Oh, come on, Rick. I don't believe that for a second." She was trying to make me feel better.

"It's true. I've never had a girlfriend." There was a weighty silence as we both sat on my bed, my hand still on her thigh.

"Have you ever been with a woman?" Lizzie faced me as she asked and my stomach spasmed.

Don't answer that. You don't want her to know you're a virgin. She'll leave when she finds that out.

Nervous and knock-kneed, I pulled my hand from hers and got up from the bed. I turned away from Lizzie. I couldn't face her as I revealed the truth about how lonely I'd been with a nonexistent sex-life.

"No. No, I've never had sex with a woman."

I can't believe I told her. I must sound so stupid, and pathetic. As much as my truth pained me, I felt she deserved to know. I didn't ever want to lie to her.

Lizzie got up from the bed, stood behind me squishing the lime-green carpet with her naked toes, and rested her head on the back of my shoulder. She placed her hand on the top of my head and casually ran her fingers through my hair. Her touch calmed me and made me feel secure, which I wasn't used to.

"Turn around, Rick," she said firmly as she forced me to face her. "You have nothing to be ashamed of. Really. There's nothing wrong with you." Lizzie whispered soothing words before she leaned in to kiss me.

She pressed her lips firmly against mine, and I felt her tongue lick along my lips and slowly enter my mouth. My eyes were open wide as our tongues intertwined and I watched myself kissing Lizzie.

Oh. My. God. It's happening. With a vampire… What if she bites me?

I pulled from her, breaking the kiss to look in her eyes. We stared at each other and I felt like I had known her forever. I never wanted to stop looking at her.

"Rick, I want you to make love to me," she whispered in my ear. "I want to be your first," she said seductively as she began to softly blow in my ear.

Fuck. This is real. Here we go.

Immediately the vision of her and Christo together came

flooding back and I paused.

"Lizzie, I really want to do this. I really, really want to. But I can't get the thought of you fucking Christo out of my head."

Lizzie turned from me and quietly said, "It's only sex, Rick."

She was right. It was only sex, and it was something that I had been wanting to experience for a long time. The circumstances had never been right, until now.

So there I was, sitting alone on my bed with a sexy, kind, sweet vampire who wanted me, and I was stuck on her past. I had no right to judge her. What was I thinking? I wanted her in spite of being nervous about whatever was going to happen — it was my first time and I wanted to embrace the experience, whatever it was.

"There's nothing to be worried about. Not Christo or anything. Honestly. I was shot in the chest at the local bar just after my eighteenth birthday and an army general saved me by turning me into a vampire. At that point I hadn't been with a man so, in a way, it's like I'm a virgin, too."

She was clearly trying to put me at ease, make me feel more comfortable. I was sorely tempted to press her for more details on how she could possibly 'qualify' as a virgin — I guess I didn't want her experience to highlight my own fear of inadequacy. I wanted her to reassure me that we were not as mismatched as I'd thought, and I wanted her to reassure me that she wouldn't laugh at me. I wanted to be with her so badly that something jealous and primal within me was beating its caveman chest.

"Okay, so you were a virgin when you died. I understand that. But what I don't understand is how that makes you a virgin now?" I knew that I was raising my voice but I felt like we were going in fucking circles.

Lizzie waited a moment again before she answered me. "Rick, my past is not what defines me, okay? I'm here now, and I want you. I showed up at your window soaking wet, for fuck's sake. And now I'm sitting with you on your bed in one of your t-shirts. I'm comfortable with you... I can't ever remember a time I've felt so at ease. Please — I want you to be comfortable, too. My experience is like a bonus, not the whole story."

"How... experienced are you?" I asked, surprising myself. Part of me wanted dirty details as the thought of her being extremely experienced really turned me on, but also made me very nervous. I really didn't want to be a disappointment.

Lizzie grabbed my hand and set it on her knee, then slowly slid my hand up her thigh and underneath the t-shirt I let her borrow. I could feel the edge of her panties brushing against my fingers. I wanted to feel her skin, her joints, her insides, but I was too nervous to move.

Lizzie tipped my head to the side and kissed my neck below my ear. *Please don't bite me. Please don't bite me. Please don't bite me.* "I'm not going to bite you, Rick. And it's okay if you want to sit here talking, but it's also more than okay if you want me to show you what experience feels like."

I didn't know where to put my hands so I kept one against her skin under her shirt, and set the other on her lower back. "What are you going to show me?" I asked as I pulled her closer and started to have a hard time breathing. If we were going any further, I was at risk of hyperventilating.

Lizzie smiled before she leaned me back to pin me down

on the bed as she reached for the zipper on my pants. "Relax, Rick. Just breathe. Breathe and try to stay calm."

"But what are you going to do?" I asked her again. I was fixated on her telling me what she had planned.

She whispered softly in my ear, "I'm going to fuck you, Rick. We're going to fuck each other. And you are going to love it."

Chapter Eleven

I could still hear the rain pounding on the window panes and the splash from passing cars, but all my attention was focused on Lizzie. She was looking at me from the foot of my bed as I laid on my back, staring at her. I didn't want to blink in case I missed something — I wanted to remember every moment.

She slowly pulled the oversized t-shirt I'd lent her up her thighs while staring intently at me. She bit her bottom lip.

Her lips look so soft and delicious. I want them all over my body.

She stopped when the bottom hem of the shirt was resting on her hips, just below her waist. I could see her perfect thighs and her black lace thong with a thin, red, satin trim that barely covered up her lady parts, which I could tell were smoothly shaven. I looked at the soft skin of her inner thighs and her lower belly, and the delicate black fabric of her panties and I wanted to lunge forward, kissing every part of her within reach. I desperately wanted to see her without anything on — what she looked like without anything covering her womanhood. It seemed a shame, and unfair that she would keep something so beautiful and perfect hidden. I had an idea of what she was going to smell and taste like, but was dying to know for sure.

She's perfect. And in my bed. Fuck the rest of the world.

Lizzie was still perched over me on her knees. She ran her

hands along her body as her eyelids fluttered, before gently rubbing herself through her panties. Her fingers massaged from north to south along the thong, pausing to massage and tap on her clit through the fabric. Slowly at first, then she began to move her fingers faster on herself and quietly moan. One of her fingers disappeared underneath her thong as she slipped it inside herself with ease. There were guttural, deeply human sounds coming from her as she touched herself just out of my reach. The volume of her moans got louder, and louder.

"I want you to touch me like this, Rick. I want your fingers inside me." She rubbed herself harder and moaned and squealed as she slipped her finger in and out of herself. She bucked and then doubled over with a yelp as she brought herself to orgasm. Panting and sweaty, she raised her eyes to meet my wondered gaze, and breathlessly said, "Oh, Rick. Please. Take me. Right now. Fuck me."

I... Is this really happening? Am I actually about to fuck this dream girl? I crave her.

"I want you to kiss me, right here," she said as she scratched her long finger along the damp black fabric of her panties. With her other hand she was gently squeezing her breasts and tapping her nipples. "I need to feel you inside me, Rick. Run your tongue over me. Put your cock inside me." She was practically purring.

Lizzie then crawled forward on the bed, licking her bottom lip and quietly whimpering. Her tongue slowly flicked at each side of her mouth and I wanted her to lick me like that, for us to lick each other.

I want her. I crave her. Please don't let this be a dream...

She ran her hands lightly up my calves, then over my knees and began to gently rub my thighs through my jeans toward the bulge in my pants. My dick was throbbing so intensely I was sure she could see it pulsating through my pants. I hoped she was impressed.

Impressed? Who am I kidding…

"Are you ready to make love, Rick? Are you ready to fuck?" Her questions echoed in my head as she reached for my waist and slowly unzipped my pants. "I've wanted you from the first time I saw you." She wrestled with the zipper over my rock-hard cock.

This is excruciating… I mean, amazing… God, I hope she's not teasing me.

I wanted her more than I'd ever wanted anything, and I wanted my first time to be with her. Desperately. Just hearing her say the word 'fuck' was driving me wild.

"I'm ready. I'm so ready for this, Lizzie. But — God! — I'm fucking terrified." I felt vulnerable and immediately regretted being honest. My heart was thumping so hard I thought it was going to burst through the walls of my chest and fall to the floor.

There are worse ways to go, but only a chump would die from a heart attack while having sex with a vampire. Come on, Rick, try to calm down.

Lizzie rubbed and massaged my skin, running her hands along my chest to help relax me while she steadied her breathing.

"What are you afraid of?" she asked as she kissed my neck. Her mouth on my neck was the best thing I'd ever felt, and it sent waves of tingles across my whole body, reverberating in my crotch. She kissed my neck again and my cock jumped. She gently bit my earlobe and my cock jumped again. I was worried one more kiss would push me over the edge before I'd even touched her.

Don't. Don't cum yet. Think about... puppies... grapefruit... apples... oranges... APPLES... ORANGES...

I was concentrating so hard on not cumming that the moment was nearly broken. And in my temporary clarity I wondered if her kissing my neck was a different kind of foreplay — the vampire kind, which would lead to her biting me, draining me of my blood and ultimately ending my life.

She's not going to bite you, so calm down. Don't be a jackass. Cowboy up and tell her what you're afraid of, then just lean in, man.

I groaned loudly before stammering, "What if I disappoint you? I, I don't want you to think I'm a disappointment... You know, because this is my first time." I was again shocked by my own honesty. "What if I'm bad at sex? What if I can't get you — you know — all the way there? What if you don't like it?"

What is this? Twenty fucking questions?

I knew my rapid-fire questions made me sound like a nervous teen, which made me feel even more exposed. But with her I couldn't seem to control the filter between my brain, and my mouth.

"You don't ever need to worry about that. This is exactly what I want. You... You are what I want. Your touch, your scent, your taste — I crave everything about you. I want you for you, Rick, not your sexual proficiency," she reassured me. "I want you to lay back, and relax. We're going to enjoy each other. You don't have to worry about a damn thing. I promise."

Her words helped pull me back to the reality of the moment. I wasn't dreaming, after all. I tried not to focus on the fact that until three weeks ago I was just a loser who couldn't get a date if I'd tried. Now the sexiest vampire in the world was on top of me, begging to make love.

I'm ready. Let's do this, baby.

Lizzie kissed my neck again and started undoing the buttons on my shirt, starting with the top. She pinched my shirt tightly between two of her fingers and smoothly slid it off my shoulders and down my back. She wrapped her arms around me to pull me close and I instinctively wrapped my arms around her, too, and we laid in an embrace. I'd never felt a woman's body against my own, and her skin was cool, soft, and smooth. She began rubbing my chest again and kissing me, this time on my mouth.

I slid my hands up and down her back, rubbing her gently. I wanted to touch every inch of her with every inch of me.

She ran her fingers through my hair, and gently scratched my scalp as she did. Every touch from her was sending shockwaves through my system. I was pinned underneath her as she pressed her legs down on mine, and I could feel my body giving in to the moment and to her. I could feel myself let go of control. I was vulnerable, but I wasn't afraid. She could do whatever she wanted with me, but I didn't feel like I was her prey.

She slowly kissed the middle of my chest as her hands slid down to my belt. I could hear the clasp come undone in between the sounds of her lips and tongue smacking and slurping my chest. Lizzie used one of her claws to cut through my pants around my zipper and gave them a tug. In an instant I was laying under her in just my boxers.

Does she think that I am good looking? Why the hell is she doing this with me? She could have anyone she wanted...

She stopped kissing my chest and looked into my eyes.

"Do you like this? Do you want me?" She reached down and touched my ever-hardening cock with her fingertips through the fabric of my shorts. Then she grasped my dick tightly in her hand tight as she rubbed up and down, up and down. "It certainly feels like you want me."

God, it feels so much better when someone else does that.

"You feel great in my hand. You're bigger than I'd imagined." Lizzie smiled as she continued to rhythmically stroke my shaft.

She imagined my dick? If she weren't about to fuck me I'd come right now.

My boxers were pulled down, and then totally off. She took them off one foot, then the other. My erection stood straight like a tower, and Lizzie stared at me.

"I'm going to put you in my mouth now, Rick. Is that all right?" she asked while holding my cock in her hand. Up and down, top to bottom, she continued to stroke me. Again, I had to use all my concentration to stop myself from exploding all over her hand right then.

What... She's going to what?

"I'm going to suck your dick, Rick. Are you okay with that?"

Shit... what... she's doing that mind reading thing. So: yeah. I think that'd be all right.

"Okay. That sounds good. Really good." I didn't want to sound too eager, which was hard.

Lizzie kissed the base of my shaft as she bent my dick back toward my stomach. She slowly worked her way up my girth and I clenched handfuls of sheets in each hand. She reached the top of my tower and took all of my erection completely in her mouth. Her lips were wrapped around my cock, tight like a glove, and her tongue flicked over the head of my penis.

This was a first for me. After weeks of mind-expanding experiences, this was my favorite so far. By far. I was in heaven. I'd never done any of this before, and I wanted her to keep initiating me.

She slid her mouth down my shaft and forced me deep into the back of her throat, almost to the base. Without thinking, I put my hand on the back of her head and guided her downward. I pushed her head further down onto my cock, forcing her nose into my stomach just below my belly button. She seemed willing, and eager. I rubbed the back of her head as she took my cock deeper and deeper, all of the way down to the back of her throat like it was nothing. Her hair weaved around every one of my fingers.

"Take off your shirt," I ordered. The words flew out of my mouth, and I was shocked at how forceful I felt with Lizzie.

Did I just tell her to take off her shirt? Another first. I really like it.

I had never told a woman to take off a piece of clothing before. Truthfully, I didn't think I'd ever told a woman to do anything before.

ABlizzie took me out of her mouth and looked up at me. Her eyes were changing from their normal ocean-blue to some unusual shade of red. I wondered if I was hallucinating in my ecstasy.

"I thought you'd never ask," she smiled at me. She pulled my baggy t-shirt over her head and revealed her flawless body. Perfection. She let me drink her in with my eyes. Her tattoos were hummingbirds of all colors, with black roses twining up her side. Her navel was pierced with a curvy, silver stud that was so shiny and clean I could almost see my own reflection in it.

But I couldn't stop admiring her breasts. They were even and round and pert like oranges, her soft pink nipples dead-center. She looked statuesque, and I desperately wanted her heft in my mouth. Her body truly was a work of art.

"I'm on fire for you, Rick... I'm so wet," she purred as she stared at me with her blood-red eyes. "So, should we fuck?" she asked me insistently. She was obviously eager.

I was desperate to feel myself inside her but wanted my cock back in her mouth first. I had never felt anything so incredible before and I needed more. Just for a minute or two.

"We are definitely going to fuck. God, yes. But could you suck, uh, it a little bit more first? Please?" I was losing my nerve, afraid she would think me greedy and would say no. And I knew that I still sounded like a horny teenager, but I didn't care. Not at all. All I wanted was my cock in her mouth. But Lizzie was still on her knees on top of me so she began rubbing my cock between the soft heft of her perfect tits.

Oh yeah, just like that. Rub against me with those beautiful nipples.

"Don't ask me. Tell me what you want me to do to you," she said. She licked my tip to tease me. "Or you get nothing," she smiled at me.

She sounded like Laura when she was alive, which kind of turned me on, in a strange way. I was trying to muster up the courage to be more assertive, to tell her what I wanted when she started to reach for her shirt in frustration.

Out with it! It's now or never. Tell her you want her to suck your dick!

"I want you to suck my dick!" I practically shouted. "I

want you to put all of my dick down your throat, as far back as you can, and then swallow."

Good job. You got it out. Now lay back; it's really happening.

Though I was surprised by my own words Lizzie must have liked them because before I knew it, my cock was back in her mouth as she writhed on top of me, shirtless.

YES.

She shoved her head down so that my member brushed the back of her throat, just like I'd demanded, and it was all I could do to not blow my load right then. I reached down and gently pinched her nipple and I listened to a moan escape her mouth as it was stuffed with my dick. I gently squeezed her breast while her tongue massaged the head of my erection again. Her fingers rubbed the base of my shaft in a circular motion. She carefully rubbed my balls and looked up to say something.

Just... Hold... On... Rick...

"I want you inside me Rick, and I don't mean just my mouth." She pulled down her black and red thong to reveal her smooth pussy to me. She began rubbing herself again as she begged me, "Please, Rick. Put your cock inside me. I am so ready for you."

A sentence I never thought I'd hear.

"Yes. I'm ready. You can let me in." I was ready, and wanting her.

Lizzie threw her leg over my body so she was straddling my lap. She kissed me hard and grinded her sex against my still-hard cock and I felt like I was in heaven. Her touch, and her smell, and her juices brought me to Nirvana. Her moaning, her skin, her perfect nakedness, were changing my life.

Lizzie poised herself two inches above my cock and grabbed it firmly. My blood was rushing to my member, visually throbbing with anticipation of the coup de grace. My breathing was fast and shallow — each inhale quicker than the last, yet I had never felt more alive. Lizzie began to lower herself onto me, guiding my cock smoothly into her before sitting down forcefully. She gripped me with her insides and winced a little as she pushed me in her further. I wrapped my arms around her naked body to get her as close to me as possible. She moved her body up and down my rod, over and over again. I could feel her claws slowly extending into my back and it hurt, but I wanted more — I wanted her to keep clawing at me like an animal, each scratch deeper and more painful than the one before. I grimaced with the pain but had never felt more alive. More real. More masculine. It was momentous; Lizzie moaned in my ear, and I whined back in hers uncontrollably.

"I want you to bite me," I whispered without fully appreciating what I'd just requested of my vampire lover. She didn't react except to fuck me even faster and harder than before. "I want you to bite me. And I want you to keep doing this," I said again.

What am I doing asking a vampire to bite me? I must have lost my mind.

Lizzie stopped riding me and sat on my hips, my organ still inside of her. I could feel her pelvic muscles tighten and pulsate around my cock. She kissed me and looked directly in my eyes.

"Are you sure?" she asked me earnestly. "I could hurt you. I could kill you." Lizzie put her head on my shoulder, right above my heart. "I don't ever want to hurt you," she said sadly.

"Sometimes I can't control how much I drink. You're going to taste amazing, and I don't want to risk losing control and then it's too late... After all, the better the blood, the more I drink."

How do I convince her to bite me?

"Please. I want to feel as close to you as possible. I want you to do this: Bite me." It felt like I was trying to convince her, and myself. But something inside me was calling out for her to bite me.

She stared at me for a moment before responding, "Okay. I'll do it. But under one condition."

"Whatever it is, I'll do it," I offered eagerly, desperately. "I will bite you." Lizzie paused. "If you bite me, too." *Why would I want to bite you?*

"Because humans get the same high from vampire blood that vampires get from humans," she said, answering my interior query. She started to ride me again. She moved her body up and down and I tried to match her motion. I was awkward and interrupted her rhythm so instead laid back, feeling the grooves on my organ slip in and out of her soft flesh. The feeling of being inside her almost made me forget about wanting her to bite me, but not completely.

"Is it going to hurt?" I whispered in her ear as she continued to wriggle on top of me.

"Only for a second, but you need to understand something: if, for any reason, I can't control myself and I drink too much of your blood, you will die." She was still moving back and forth on my cock while explaining the risks, which was incredibly hot. "If that happens, as long as I can get my blood in your system before you die, you could come back as a vampire," she moaned as she fucked me harder.

So I'd be like you? Yes. Yes. Yes. Why wouldn't I want to

be like you?

"Do you understand? Do you still want this, Rick?" It was clear Lizzie wanted me to appreciate the risks, and wanted me to be sure.

Up until then my life had felt meaningless, empty. Since I first saw her three weeks ago, Lizzie had quickly and easily become the best thing that ever happened to me. If I were to become a vampire, I could spend the rest of eternity with her. I knew that forever was a long time, but even that wasn't enough time to spend with her.

"Bite me, beautiful," I said. I reached down and tentatively ran my fingers around her nethers. I wanted to know what she felt like and started to rub around her clit with my thumb. I wasn't sure what I should be doing, but it was almost like my instincts took over when it came to getting her off. She screamed in pleasure and rocked against my hand then brought her wrist to her mouth. I watched as she forced her own fangs deep into her skin. "Don't stop. Rub me harder. Yes. Yes. More!" She screamed as her fangs pierced her skin and blood dripped from her mouth and trickled onto her right breast. I watched the drops of blood run from her breast, down her abdomen, to mingle with her sex, and mine.

Lizzie pressed her pierced wrist against my mouth. "Drink," she said. I suckled once at her wrist and her blood came gushing into my mouth, where it felt hot and thick and tasted sweet. Like the most exotic, refined strawberry juice in the world. Instantly I felt light-headed, but then my pupils dilated and my eyes narrowed on Lizzie, like I was seeing her for the first time: her hair had never been so blonde, the inks in her tattoos were brighter, and I clearly saw my face in her navel ring. Except in the vision of myself, I had fangs like hers.

It felt like I was even deeper inside her but still wanted to push further. Every one of my senses was heightened to the max.

This. Is. Awesome.

"Don't ever stop fucking me!" My mouth spit out the words before I knew what I was saying. "Bite me. Bite me now," I pleaded. I didn't care if it was going to hurt.

Lizzie kept riding me. I was in heaven. Her blood still stained my lips and my head swam.

"Yes, I'm going to bite you." Just as she answered her eyes turned bright red. Then her front incisors grew long so they hung down over her bottom lip. They were so sharp they practically glinted, and suddenly I was afraid and didn't want to be bitten.

Stay calm. It's all right. If you die you'll just come back as a vampire, which wouldn't be a tragedy.

Lizzie leaned her head forward like she was going to rest it on my shoulder as she continued to grind and pump on top of me. I focused on her womanhood swallowing my member over and over rather than the set of gleaming fangs poised by my jugular. Then I felt her razor-sharp fangs pierce my neck. The pain was sharp, but quick — nothing like the claws she'd been digging into my back since climbing on top of me. Her fangs pressed deeper into my flesh until I felt the blood start to leave my body. Just as it flowed, Lizzie suckled from my neck as her hips bucked wildly and she started fucking me even harder. Like an animal.

It felt amazing. All of it. The sex, her sucking my blood, me drinking hers. The combination was unreal. I wanted her to keep going forever but I could feel myself getting close to cumming — I was shocked that I'd lasted as long as I had. She continued to suck from my neck and I started to feel woozy, and began to hope she was almost done drinking.

With a loud grunt at my neck Lizzie bounced up and down on me with brute force to fuck me with all of the strength within her. I couldn't hold it in any longer so I exploded with a volcanic force inside her and roared. Lizzie kept thrusting as I came. "Oh, Rick. Yes. Fuck, Rick. Yes, harder!" She shuddered, screamed, then sighed and began to slow down.

"How was that for you, handsome?" Lizzie asked. She ran her fingers through my hair. I was euphoric from her blood, and awash in the afterglow. I laid my head back and closed my eyes and could feel her quivering against me. I was tired and weak, and needed to sleep.

"It was absolutely amazing," I answered with my eyes still closed.

"Good." She moved towards my neck again.

"I don't think you should take any more from me... Lizzie... I already don't feel good," I said as I limply tried to fend her off.

"It's all right," she said. "You just taste so damn good. I just want a little bit more. I need more of you."

I could feel her fangs pierce the skin on the back of my neck, next to the existing punctures. I felt weaker by the second and my vision was narrowing, getting blurry. I felt like I was leaving my body; I knew I was fading, and it was hard to keep my eyes open. The last thing I saw was a blue hummingbird on her stomach flit past my eyes. I blacked out as she bit me again.

Chapter Twelve

The sunlight pouring through the windows nearly blinded me when I woke. Lizzie was sitting next to me. When my eyes focused, I saw that she was fully dressed in her now-dry clothes, evidently waiting for me to wake. She looked amazing, as always, though I missed how sexy she'd looked in my dopey t-shirt the night before. I'd never considered my clothes sexy before, but she transformed them.

Sexy. Another first.

I had moved through my thirty-six years without ever being called sexy. Laura — now Dead Laura — hit on me all the time but that always felt more mean, than alluring. 'Undesired' had been one of my defining qualities up until now.

Everything was extremely fuzzy, and not just because I wasn't wearing my glasses. I moved my hand to the side of my neck and ran my fingers over the tiny holes from where Lizzie had bitten me. The pain surged instantly as I brushed against my open wounds. I shifted my hand to the back of my neck and could feel another set of sore puncture wounds.

Goddamn, that hurts...

I winced in pain as I looked out at the brick building across the alley outside my bedroom window. I was home. I was groggy but realized some part of me had wished I'd be waking in a secret lair, or velvet-draped boudoir. A cave, even.

Just something different from my little grey apartment. I'd wanted to wake completely transformed from my first night of lovemaking, especially since it was with Lizzie, my newfound mythical creature.

Shit. Well, nothing like wishful thinking.

I turned to Lizzie, and she greeted me with her perfect smile. She was holding my hand, gently rubbing my knuckles with her thumb. I sat up faster than I should have and was met with a throbbing pain in the middle of my forehead.

Everything fucking hurts.

"Easy, tiger. You had quite a work out last night," she said, laying me back down. I didn't resist. "You probably feel like you've got a severe hangover — that's normal when so much blood leaves your body. You need to eat and drink. Lots of fluids, handsome. Just like when you're sick."

I have a lifetime's worth of experience with hangovers — this is something different. The pain was much more intense, and so much worse. This was not some run-of-the-mill hangover caused by too much bottom shelf gin.

Broken, incomprehensible images from the night before were flashing in my brain. Like small movie clips playing before my eyes. Then I remembered her sucking on my body. And then her fucking me. And then I wanted to keep watching the clips replay in mind, basking in the glory that was my first time.

I remembered begging her to bite me, and her eventually agreeing. She warned me. It was a ludicrous request, but she had come back for a second helping after I'd asked her not to. Then there was nothing; just a sharp pain in my neck and then everything went black.

"Maybe I wouldn't have such an ungodly headache if you

hadn't drunk so much of my fucking blood," I snapped, like a dick.

She began to explain. "I didn't—" but I interrupted.

"What do you mean you didn't? You didn't what? Kill me? Is that what you didn't do?" I wasn't sure why I was so angry with her, and didn't have enough sense to be fucking gracious. After all, she was doing what I'd asked. She'd done what I wanted. I was probably snapping at her because I felt so terrible; I was sweaty and I'm sure that I smelled horrible. I was feeling shitty, and acting shitty. I needed to shower.

"No," she said as she folded her arms She looked away from me and continued, "I didn't mean to drink more than I should have. I told you it's almost impossible to control how much I drink. Let alone from someone who tastes so damn good. You are so sweet."

Sweet?

She got up from the bed, and walked over to the window.

No crazy vampire speed now?

"But that's no excuse and I'm really sorry," she said, staring out the window. "If it makes you feel any better, I only drank a few drops the second time 'round. I could feel your pulse weaken in my mouth, and could tell you were fading, but I couldn't stop. It was nearly impossible for me to pull myself from your neck… You might be the best I've ever tasted."

I seriously must have a death wish.

"How… What made you stop drinking from me?" I was grumpy and suspicious, but liked hearing her talk about how sweet I tasted. I'd never felt so complimented and wanted more of it from her.

She said that I tasted good… Hmmm. I couldn't stop her, so how was she able to stop herself?

"Honestly? I could hear your heart slowing and your breathing was very shallow. I didn't want to kill you. I... I didn't think I could live with that. I have loved each and every minute of the little bit of time we've had together." She sighed, still looking out the window, then offered, "Not to mention I had a pretty good time with you last night." She finally turned to me, and smiled. "And it wouldn't be as good with you dead. Trust me."

She enjoyed last night? Like, the sex? With me? And my dick? The sex with me and my dick?

Lizzie laughed out loud and replied, unprompted, "Yes, I really enjoyed the sex. With you and your dick," she said, walking back to the bed.

"I wish I could control which thoughts you heard as they run through my head. The inside of my head can feel pretty scary..." I groaned as I sat up and said, "You never know what's going to come popping out at you when you're in there." I grabbed my glasses from the nightstand, and the room snapped into focus when I put them on. I didn't need glasses to see Lizzie's beauty, though — a blind man could have seen her coming.

"So, is there some secret remedy for a horrible headache brought on by an acute loss of blood?" I asked, massaging my temples.

You know, from a run-in with a vampire?

"This pain is really rough," I added. I had gotten pretty good at nursing a typical hangover but suspected that a strong cup of coffee or energy drink wouldn't do the trick this time. I had no idea how to deal with a vampire hangover.

I blinked and was suddenly alone in my bedroom — Lizzie was gone. But with a gust of wind, she was back, standing directly in front of me holding a plate loaded with two slices of buttered toast and a cup of pinkish juice. A bottle of Tylenol was balanced on the plate next to the dark brown toast.

Goddamn, she is fast.

"Wow, that was quick," I said, still amazed by her speed. "I'll eat the toast, but what is that pink stuff? I usually just make a pot of super strong coffee after a night of hard drinking. If you can stomach it, it works wonders." I groaned as I sat up straighter. "Coffee can be a magical bean when it's brewed properly. Do I really have to drink that?" I asked as I pointed to the glass of pink-hued, God knows what.

Lizzie handed me the plate. I took a bite of the toast, and reveled in her ability to get the perfect amount of butter evenly spread from edge to edge.

Just one more thing she can do perfectly. Dream girl. She was the total package.

She shook two Tylenol in my hand and pushed the juice towards me, offering it insistently. "Drink it. It'll make you feel better. It's just orange juice," she said cheerfully. "With a bit of a kick." She winked. "And I'm here with you right now, baby — I'm no dream," she said with a lilting laugh.

"A kick? Is that why it's pink?" I was feeling both skeptical and nauseated.

"It has a few drops of my blood in it," she said breezily. "It's fine. A nip from the hair of the dog, as they say?"

That logic works, anyway. I've been known to take a sip of gin on the way to work. Whatever it takes...

I reluctantly grabbed the cup of juice. I popped the two Tylenol in my mouth and took a big gulp from the glass to wash down the pills. It tasted like orange juice, but a hint sweeter. It didn't taste like her blood from what I half-remembered. But if drinking more of her blood this morning would get my head in shape to deal with everything else going on — namely,

Christo — then I could deal.

"That'll make you feel better, but will also help restore your strength. Sometimes a few drops can make all the difference," she said. I tipped the glass and finished the bloody cocktail in two gulps. "What do you have planned for today? Anything fun and exciting?" she asked.

I've had more than enough fun and excitement lately, thank you very much. I'd gotten my fill even before a thousand-year-old vampire started using New York City like his playground.

I finished the toast and wiped the crumbs from my mouth with my wrist. "I'm going to head to the café to tell Paul about the bodies in his back alley. He's going to have to call the police, or clean it up somehow. And... And then I guess I should ask Maryanne how to deal with Christo. Someone needs to do something."

I hated saying the villain's name, or even thinking about him. He was a murderous, blood-sucking, flesh-eating, vampiric demon who had to be stopped. By any means necessary.

"I'd like to go with you to the café. I — I saw what he did to that couple in the alley. I've tried stopping him so many times, but it's not possible. Not on my own," Lizzie said. "I came to you, Rick, after what Christo did to those people last night. I'll tell Paul and Maryanne what happened, and that I tried stopping him. I don't think that Paul trusts me, but if I come forward it might prove to everyone how bad I really want to stop Christo."

She had come to me. Straight to me, soaking wet, after fighting Christo. She dragged me deeper into The Other World and I had yelled at her about it. Shouted at her out of fear, and still she embraced me.

"Uh, yeah. You can come with me. Can't hurt," I answered a little too casually. "But it's early morning — won't the sun turn you to ash?" Thinking back on it, I'd only ever seen her in the morning until last night. I was no expert, but I thought the sun was the last stop for vampires. "The sun is supposed to roast you, right? Isn't it like your Kryptonite?" Lizzie smiled as she tossed me my jeans.

"You'll need these if we're going anywhere, sun or no. Just because I enjoy you without pants doesn't mean you're to everyone's taste." She added, "Plus, I don't like to share."

I pulled the comforter back and felt the fabric shift against my good-morning erection. I ignored it and stood up to put my jeans on and realized that my headache was completely gone — another new sensation.

A few drops of vampire blood is all you need for a hangover? GOT IT.

Good to know. Now, if only we could do something about this boner...

"That's all you need," she answered my thoughts. "And as far as your boner? We don't have time for that right now." She squeezed my hip and whispered, "But there's always tonight."

It was almost painful tearing myself from her, but we needed to get to the café to give Paul a heads-up to last night's bloodbath in his back alley. And hopefully without drawing attention from any of his customers. We had to beat the breakfast rush.

"I'm never going to get used to that little mind reading trick of yours,"

I said, "But… about the sun — Isn't it going to be a problem for you?" I pulled up my jeans and looked around for my belt.

I should get some more vampire blood if I'm gonna keep drinking — that stuff works like a charm.

"Normally, yes. The sun will end us. Burned to a crisp. But I don't have to worry about that." she said conspiratorially.

"And why is that? You have more tricks up your sleeve?" I teased.

"I have some tricks, Rick. Yes, I do. But this is more of a special favor someone did for me a very long time ago. I have a special ring."

A special ring?

"Yes, an enchanted ring. A very powerful witch found me just after I was turned. I was still learning, and she helped me learn how to control my cravings; how to exist as a vampire. It's very easy to give into the urges and just become, well, a monster. Human blood is addicting, especially for a new vampire: it's impossible to control the need for human blood. But when you give into it and kill, the cravings only get worse. So, the witch helped me learn to control myself. She helped me survive. I once asked her why she helped me and she said that, even though I had been turned into a monster, she was able to see that my soul was pure. And that I wasn't evil.

"She helped me understand that the threat of becoming a monster is always there, but I don't have to be trapped by it. She showed me I don't have to live in the shadows forever. And to help me she put a spell on this ring that allows me to walk in the daylight whenever I'm wearing it. I only wear it when I have to, so it's out of sight most of the time. If other vampires found out about it, they would try to take it from me. If they knew of this ring's power, they would definitely be willing to kill, or die for it." She paused and looked at me as I was processing everything she'd just said. My eyes were practically crossing.

"Wow. Well, that's something. I'm glad you can go out in the sun without becoming a pile of ash." I looked in the mirror for one final, disappointing look.

"Me too," she said.

"Does Christo know? I can't imagine him knowing would be a good thing, right?"

"He's the only one who does, actually. But it's only because I've spent so much time with him. Honestly, there's no way he could've missed it," she said, her words heavy with connotations, "but he's never taken it because he doesn't need it because the sun doesn't kill him. I'm convinced he really is immortal."

Great...

I was still looking at my reflection while she was talking, but I only saw myself in the mirror. I spun around quickly to catch her missing but there she was, still standing in the corner of my room. "Huh. So, vampires don't have a reflection either?" I asked stupidly. I was still new to all of the vampire rules.

"You've never heard of that before? You really are sheltered. Vampires can only see their own reflections. Just another perk, I guess. A way for us to stay hidden from humans," Lizzie offered sardonically. "You've never seen Dracula? Or any of those teenage vampire dramas? Granted, most of them are the trashiest representations ever. I mean, seriously. We sparkle in the sun? Really? No. We're done. Become nothing more than a pile of burnt ash." I could tell it was a touchy subject for her.

I looked outside and could see from the leaves whirling past my window that the wind was picking up. Mother Nature was mighty fickle in New York; it could be sunny and warm one day, then cold and snowy the next. Especially in the fall.

"So you're coming with me to Paul's?" I asked, changing the subject so I didn't have to keep admitting how little I actually knew about vampires. I grabbed a hoodie from my closet and made for the door.

"Yeah, I'll meet you there."

"That's fine. I think I'm actually gonna take a quick shower before I head out," realizing I had put all my clean clothes over my stinking post-coital body.

Ugh.

I was still out of it.

"Did you forget that you had to shower?" Lizzie asked. She pulled down the zipper, then my pants off in one swift motion.

"This brings back memories," she said playfully. "Good memories."

She slid my boxers down so I was standing naked and then reached for my quickly hardening erection.

"Don't tease — That's not nice. We don't have time for you to finish the job." I brushed her hands away from my cock.

"You're right," she agreed. "Sorry." She stepped away. "You go get cleaned up and I'll meet you at Paul's."

Is she always so understanding?

"Sounds good to me, gorgeous."

Gorgeous? Did I just call a girl gorgeous? Another first.

Lizzie leaned in close and kissed my cheek with a level of intimacy I'd never known. It was totally foreign, and I totally loved it. I wanted to get used to having her around.

"Enjoy your shower, handsome. I'll see you in a few minutes." There was a small gust of wind and she was gone, and I didn't think she'd be back with toast and a bloody cocktail this time.

She left, and I was crestfallen. I could feel myself growing attached to her — a non-living, beautiful female vampire. Though I knew I'd be seeing her again in a few short minutes, I already missed her.

I needed to shower so I made my way down my very short hallway to get to my very small bathroom. The shower was just big enough to stand in next to the toilet, sink, and two small cabinets that were mostly empty.

I turned the bathroom light on and instinctively turned on the shower at the same time, knowing that the water liked to take its sweet time getting hot. Beggars, choosers, small bathroom users.

The joys of being broke. Though now maybe I'll finally get a promotion since Laura is, er, dead.

It was hard being gracious and generous and broke at the same time; I didn't want to think ill of the dead, but I also had bills to pay. I turned to look at myself in my mirror and the surface was beginning to fog from the shower's steam.

Finally! This damned thing takes forever to heat up.

I stepped into the shower and let the hot water hit the top of my head and slowly run down my body. I could feel my muscles begin to loosen one by one and I began to relax. I squeezed a dollop of shampoo into my palm and started to massage it into my scalp.

I was reminded of how Lizzie had rubbed me all over the night before. I rubbed my head in circles, the same way she had rubbed my chest and other parts. Up and down the back of my neck, just like she had done.

But I needed to focus.

I finished rinsing my hair, and I looked down to see something very strange. It looked like a face in the knob of my shower.

What the fuck?

It looked like the mouth was moving but I couldn't make out the words. I leaned in to get a closer look and was shocked that I recognized the face as something other than my own distorted reflection. It was someone familiar... Some baldheaded man.

"Lazarus!" I shouted as soon as I figured out who I was looking at. "What the hell?" I asked the head in my shower knob. His lips were moving but I couldn't hear what he was saying. After a few seconds his voice began to cut through the roar of the shower.

"Rick, help me! Please!" he begged.

"Help you with what?" Lazarus had never asked me for anything before.

"I need to warn you! I tried to warn you the first time."

I recalled our less-than-pleasant run-in in the bathroom at Lightning Pop.

That was a warning? Warn me of what?

"Christo is making me kill people. He's controlling me. I can't stop. I have to obey him. Please, help me."

What could I do to help him?

"What can I do? Tell me what to do to help you, and I'll do it!" I didn't know what else to say. I didn't know how to help him. I wasn't sure if I could.

"Just get to the café and do whatever you can to stop Christo. Please. Stop me... By any means necessary." He stopped speaking and stared.

"Wait, Lazarus! Tell me what to do!" I needed more direction, but it was no use. He was gone and I had no idea what I was supposed to do.

Fuck! How do I explain that?

I didn't think that I could. I turned off the running water and rushed out of the shower.

Paul's. Get to Paul's. Before something else happens.

I dried and dressed myself, finally ready to head out the door. I was still amazed by — and grateful for! — that little bit of vampire blood that had gotten rid of my headache. Nothing had ever worked that well for me before.

I rushed out of my apartment, down the multiple flights of stairs to the front door, then burst out my building's front door to the busy street. I was greeted by the sun beating down on me — it had never felt so warm and intense. Not too hot, just very focused.

God, that sun feels great. And not a cloud in the sky. Maybe that's a sign, things are looking up.

Chapter Thirteen

I walked down the street and pushed through the crowds of regular people hurrying through the crisp, fall air. The wind whipped and smacked me in the face with a damp leaf that stuck and clung to my glasses. I brushed it off but quickly gave up and surrendered to the wind's whims as leaves continued to pelt my face. I shielded my eyes from the sun's light, which was blinding.

Goddamn, that is bright.

I kept my eyes cast downward and tried not to focus on how badly my hands were shaking. The morning after a night of heavy drinking often left me shaky, but this was different.

Nerves? Or maybe I'm having a seizure, which would be icing on the cake right now.

Walking to Paul's Café before work, was a routine I usually found comforting, but that morning I was as distracted as I'd ever been and dreading what awaited me. I hoped the day would bring some relief, some closure once I helped Maryanne and Paul clean up the latest mess, and then hopefully they would provide some insight on how to handle Christo.

Dead couple out back. Crazed immortal vampire on a killing spree. Lazarus's face in my shower. And it's not even nine a.m.

I allowed myself to feel the full extent of my nerves,

which stopped me in my tracks. The crowd continued to push past me but I was frozen with anxiety. I was ill-equipped to handle my human problems, so was less than thrilled to have to deal with the supernatural. I hoped to God Maryanne and Paul would come up with a plan to end Christo. Someone had to.

What is Christo going to do to me when he finds out I'm involved? I don't want to die. I don't really want him to turn me, either, but I really don't want to die. Shit...

I refused to end up like Lazarus — Christo's unwilling lackey. Still frozen in thought, I turned my face skyward and felt the sun's warmth wash over my skin and radiate through my body — it had never felt so intense, so strong. I assumed I was feeling different from the sex and vampire blood — a guess, but it stood to reason.

I snapped out of it and resolved to get moving — procrastinating would only get me so far. Reluctantly, I put one foot in front of the other.

Rounding the final corner to Paul's, I was shocked to find a crowd of people gathered near the front of the café. I could barely see the doors through the crowd, which had formed a semicircle around the usually lonely entrance. I tried to make my way around the huddle of onlookers but found that the alley behind Paul's had been blocked off with yellow tape. Crime scene tape. **DO NOT CROSS**. The oversized, black letters were shouting at me to stay back, and I didn't dare defy them.

Someone must have found the dead couple in the dumpster.

My hands started to shake more violently as I pictured Christo viciously murdering the unsuspecting couple. He was a menace, and I could only hope he was the worst we had to deal with.

I craned my neck over the crowd and saw Paul by the back door talking to someone short and very chubby. The chubby man's tan trench coat was longer than he was tall, and it was dragging on the ground behind him. A black fedora was perched on his head, tipped so far to the right that it looked like the wind was going to send it flying off his head at any second.

When he finally turned around, I recognized the fat man. *Detective Lee! Shit.*

I had been avoiding him because I didn't want to answer any of his needling questions — not that I could have answered them honestly, even if I'd wanted to, which I definitely didn't.

Paul stood facing him. He lifted the grease-stained apron hanging from his neck over his head and folded it in his arms across his chest, further obscuring his sapphire necklace. Even from a distance he looked more than a little agitated.

I thought about the message Detective Lee left me a few days ago, asking if I knew anything about Laura's body being dug up. His voice replayed in my head and gave me an instantaneous headache that pounded in the middle of my forehead. Not unlike the vampire hangover I was still nursing. Maybe I should have called him back… Anyway, now he has bigger problems Like people getting mauled by blood-sucking demons.

My mind started racing, scanning my memories for infractions in case the detective wanted to have a chat.

Does… does he suspect I had something to do with Laura's body? What if he thinks I was involved in the murder of the couple in the alley? How the fuck am I supposed to explain knowing about the murders?

Just as I was going to duck out of sight of the crowd and Detective Lee, he spotted me. He pointed at me, nodded, and immediately began walking in my direction.

Shit! What do I say to him? Deny, deny, deny. You're a shit liar, Rick, so just keep your cool.

Detective Lee groaned and wheezed as he ducked under the yellow tape before standing to face me, his face now bright red.

...This is going to be really bad...

"Good morning, Mr Blume," he said in a rasp as he tried to catch his breath. "I'm glad you're here. I've been meaning to talk to you to follow up on Laura's investigation. Did you get the message I left for you a few days back?" He coughed, hacked up in his throat, then spit.

Gross. Also, what message?

I was falling at the first hurdle. Should I have lied to him, saying that I didn't get any message? Or, that I only just listened to it last night, and had planned on calling him back today, but that I'd gotten distracted spending the night with a beautiful woman? Even when I injected truth into the lie I knew it was still unbelievable.

"I actually just got it last night and was going to call you back today," I answered, trying not to make it too obvious that I was lying through my teeth.

"I understand," he said. He looked me dead in the eyes, which was awkward because he was at least six inches shorter than me. He continued, "I was wondering if you'd heard anything about Laura's grave being dug up?" He paused, which I interpreted as a tacit accusation.

I definitely can't tell him the truth about that... He can't find out I was there... I know nothing. Please leave me alone.*

I was extremely uncomfortable and anxious, but did my best.

"Dug up? Wow. No, I hadn't heard anything about that at all. Do you think they were looking for something? Or, I mean, did they take anything?" I was doing my best to sound like an innocent concerned citizen.

"The only thing they took was, well, Laura's body. Very strange. Never seen anything like it in my seventeen years as a police officer. Four years as a detective and nothing ever like it," he said, shaking his perfectly round head. It seemed like he believed my story, but I couldn't imagine what was running through his head as he found himself in the thick of a supernatural killing spree.

"They took her body?" I asked with feigned shock.

Easy, Rick. Just sound surprised. You're good at sounding stupid, so just be yourself.

"All I can say is that her body is now missing and I was wondering if you'd heard anything," he said while furrowing his brow.

They didn't actually dig her up — it was a resurrection, but you didn't hear it from me.

"I'm really sorry to hear about what happened to the grave. I hope you catch whoever was involved. It sure is strange." I hoped I was convincing enough to get him off my case, while praying he would never catch the people involved: Paul, Maryanne, and me.

Please leave us alone. Maryanne was just trying to help her. Really. And Dead Laura is fine — she's better than ever!

He must have bought it since he announced, "Oh, don't you worry, we'll get all of this sorted out. One way or another."

Just as the detective finished speaking, Paul approached us and ducked under the yellow tape the same way the fat detective had, but without the wheezing and heaving. He walked directly over and planted himself between the plump man and myself, facing me while smoking a cigarette.

"Morning, Rick." He clapped me on the shoulder and squeezed a salutation. His grip was an effective reminder that he was part wolf — maybe more wolf than human. I hadn't seen his transformation so had no idea how the process worked, but even as a man, there was clearly a lot of wolf in him.

"How's it going, Paul?" I already knew that he wasn't having a terrific morning. I tried squeezing his shoulder in kind but failed miserably as my still-shaking hands seized up, sending a throbbing pain through my fingers.

"It's been better," Paul growled. "Did Detective Lee tell you what we've got going on here this morning? It has been another eventful one."

No, but Lizzie told me everything Christo did here last night. Right before she took me to bed for the first time and blew my mind. I mean, I got to have sex with Lizzie! Can you believe that?! It was the morning after, and I was still adjusting.

The fat detective jumped in before I could answer Paul to note, "I actually hadn't got to that part yet. It seems there was a young couple murdered last night behind the café over there in the alley. A man and a woman. Both in their mid-to-late-twenties, probably," he said while gesturing toward the alley. "I've gotta say, it's pretty gruesome."

Lizzie was telling the truth.

Part of me hoped that everything my vampiric goddess

had told me about Christo's rampage was just more fantasy. But it wasn't. Everything was just as she'd described. I could see the black body bags at the foot of the dumpster where she'd stashed the corpses. I couldn't imagine the dedication it'd take to clean up after the likes of Christo. God bless the coroner.

"A couple was murdered?" I parroted innocently. "In the back alley? Do they know who did it? Or who they were? Do they know anything?" I didn't want to seem too interested in the investigation, but my nerves were letting my mouth run wild. After all, I already knew who the killer was. Rather, who the monster was.

It was that crazy vampire — Christo! God, I hope he can't read minds like Lizzie, or else I'm toast.

The detective pulled out his notepad from inside his trench coat. "Unfortunately, we don't have much to go on. The only thing we have is a name that was carved into the abdomen of the female victim. ELIZABETH. We aren't sure if that was the name of the female victim, or possibly the attacker? Hopefully we can get some traces of DNA from that. Let's hope, because there isn't much else." The detective furrowed his brow more deeply before adding, "It doesn't look like whoever did this used a knife or blade of any kind. The wounds are wide and deep and — now I'm no expert in this kind of thing — but it looks like it was done by a claw, or a talon, or something. We'll just have to wait and see what comes back from the lab."

When Detective Lee had said my vampire queen's name I felt a pang in my heart, and butterflies in my stomach. It seemed like Christo was deliberately trying to pin his murders on Lizzie, which terrified me. Hearing Lee say her name made me wonder what would happen if she were found out and revealed for what she really is. Would she be killed? Studied? Tormented? I feared for Lizzie's safety.

"I don't know anybody named Elizabeth," I replied instinctively and Paul gave me a look as he threw his cigarette to the ground. He stepped on it with his boot and ground it into the pavement.

"Neither do I," Paul said a split second after I did.

Thank you, friend. Thank you! We are bound in secrecy and I'll never tell. You have my word. Thank you, thank you. Friend.

The detective scratched his fat head and shrugged. "I didn't assume that either of you did — I just wanted to let you know what we're working with. Again, it isn't much." He seemed confused, but also like he was used to feeling confused.

"Why don't we all go inside and grab a cup of coffee and a muffin, or something, huh? Maybe then we can discuss things a little more privately. We really should get away from this crowd, which is getting nosy. They've already seen too much, if you ask me." Paul ushered us toward the front doors of his café and away from the madding crowd.

"Great idea. I'll have a couple of patrolling officers come by to disperse this crowd shortly," the detective said as he followed Paul into the dark cafe. I followed them both and shut the door behind me, leaving the onlookers to gawp and speculate in the street.

Inside the café was almost dead, as per usual. Christo sat at his regular table in the back, Lazarus at his side. I could feel them watching us, but every time I looked over at them their faces were buried in their crinkling newspapers. An old woman sat at the counter contentedly eating a chocolate chip muffin. Maryanne was nowhere in sight, unlike usual.

That's weird, Maryanne is always here. She must be dealing with Dead Laura. Fingers crossed they're not in the basement — I don't know how we'd explain Dead Laura's grunts and groans to Detective Lee here.

Lazarus finally looked at me and we locked eyes. He mouthed something silently — it looked like he was saying, "HELP ME."

How am I supposed to help him? What does he expect me to do?

The fat detective plopped himself on a stool and wiggled himself up to the counter. Paul and I sat on either side of him. Paul filled a sturdy mug with steaming black coffee from the pot to his left, and gently slid it down the counter so it landed squarely in front of me. He knew how I liked my coffee: plain, and fast.

"No cream or sugar?" the fat detective asked as he waited for Paul to give him a cup.

"Just a little sugar for me," I responded in between sips.

Maybe a little whiskey, or gin, but never cream. Yuck.

The cafe doors slammed open and Lizzie walked in, the sun streaming in behind her and illuminating her with an angelic glow. She was perfect, and from the moment I saw her I was no longer afraid. I couldn't explain it logically but she made me feel like everything was going to be all right.

Yeah, right.

Lizzie pulled up a stool to the counter and stationed herself between the old woman and myself. She didn't acknowledge Christo or Lazarus. Not even for a second.

She's incredible.

"Hey, handsome," she smiled at me. "How's it going?"

She squeezed my thigh under the counter to get my attention. Immediately I was flooded with memories from the previous night's sexual adventures. My jeans were tightening around my growing bulge so I tried to cool off, and not to think sexually, which was practically impossible when she was around.

I was careful not to mention her name in front of the fat detective so simply said, "Uh, hi. I just stopped in for a quick breakfast before work." I still hadn't been back to work since Laura had been murdered, and I legitimately needed to check in if everything stayed quiet at the café. I hoped Tony hadn't run Lightning Pop into the ground.

"Perfect," Lizzie chirped. "I could use a bite — I had a really long night." She slid her hand higher up my thigh and closer to my cock. I remembered the way she'd bitten me and almost drank me dry, and how I'd yelled at her all morning about it. Instead of breakfast I wanted to have her on the counter: languid, exposed, and all mine.

"This is Detective Lee, and you already know Paul," I said, turning towards them both, hoping to get rid of some of my sexual frustration by changing the subject, however unlikely.

"Pleasure to meet you, ma'am," the fat detective said with a tip of his ill-fitting fedora. "And what is your name?"

"This is Rick's friend, Sarah Colden." Paul jumped in immediately, yet again helping me protect her. "She's just moved here," he added, "and she's applied for the receptionist position in Rick's office."

"I couldn't believe the crowd of people gathered out front," Lizzie cut in, not missing a beat. "You must've had quite a busy morning here, Paul."

He looked behind him to give Christo a visual check, clearly clocking him as the perpetrator. "Yeah. You could say that. There's been a lot of shit going on lately. It's getting out of hand."

There was a sudden bang from the basement that echoed up through the vents. Paul and I gave each other a knowing look that we were going to have to get our stories straight on the fly. "That's probably just Maryanne," Paul shrugged, trying to convince the fat man. Then I offered, "Yeah, she's always messing around with some kind of project down there." I tried to act casual.

Whatever the bang was, at least it wasn't one of Dead Laura's unmistakable grunts, which would be harder to explain. I hadn't seen Dead Laura in days, and just hoped she wasn't about to make an appearance.

The basement door swung open and Maryanne stepped out and into the kitchen. She came towards us and stopped at the other side of the counter from Paul.

"Hey, everybody," she said to acknowledge the five of us at the counter, as she waved casually to the old woman.

Paul pointed to his right with his thumb and said, "This is Detective Lee. And you remember Rick's friend, Sarah." He nodded to Maryanne, she nodded back, and we were all on the same page; don't say anything that might make the detective suspicious.

"Yes, of course," she played along. "It's nice to see you again. Can I get anybody anything else to eat or drink this morning?" She pulled a sliced bagel from the bin behind the counter and began to smother it with cream cheese.

Detective Lee didn't miss a beat: "Please! I would love a few pieces of French toast with some bacon." He was grinning.

He wants French toast and bacon… God, get outta here, man. We don't have time for you to get your grub on.

"And maybe a glass of orange juice?" He set his wallet on the counter.

"Comin' right up!" Maryanne hurried back to the kitchen and out of sight.

The old woman at the end of the counter stopped eating her muffin mid-bite, got off her stool and headed to the back of the café toward the bathroom. Her gait was normal until she was about ten feet from Christo and Lazarus, at which point she silently marched up to their table. She bent her ear towards Christo in a stiff, unnatural way as he quickly whispered something. The old woman jerked back upright and turned to face the counter, and smiled at me. Something in her eyes was unnerving.

The woman held my gaze as she approached the counter.

Something bad is about to happen. I can feel it.

I had a horrible feeling in my gut that worsened as the woman moved closer. I watched her pick up a fork from one of the tables and slide it into the sleeve of her sweater. I didn't know what to do, and then the woman walked up behind the fat detective and tapped him on the shoulder. He turned around on his stool to face her and smiled.

"Morning, ma'am? Can I help you?"

The clatter and sizzle of Maryanne cooking nearly drowned her tiny voice as she answered, "Hello, sir. I'm Francine."

"Nice to meet you, Francine. I'm Detective Jackson Lee. What can I do for you?" he asked, more out of obligation than genuine interest.

"You can do me a favor and DIE!" Francine shrieked as

she pulled the fork from her sleeve and drove it straight into the detective's chest. He gasped as the tines pierced his sweater, shirt, undershirt, his skin, and drove through to his flesh.

Aaaaah!

Lizzie screamed and Maryanne dropped the pan in the kitchen, sending grease and pieces of eggy bread across the floor. I was in shock and didn't move. The old woman pulled the fork from the fat man's chest, then stabbed him again, and again. His chest squelched with each puncture, and his eyes were rolling wildly. She stabbed him in the neck and blood sprayed from his jugular, spattering my shoulder and coating the counter and floor.

Paul turned on his stool and immediately slammed the old woman to the floor with observable force. He pinned her to the ground with his hands.

The detective's mouth was silently opening and closing, like a fish out of water. Lizzie grabbed my hand and placed it firmly on the detective's neck. "Hold pressure on it. Lots of pressure," she instructed. "I have to get out of here before I become part of the problem." Her eyes were already starting to blaze red. "Sorry, Rick — I'll catch up with you later. Good luck." In a blink, she was gone.

Maryanne ran to me with dish towels in her hands. I put my arms around the fat man, trying to support him so he didn't fall to the floor. I pressed the towels against his beck and chest, but the blood didn't stop. A crimson spurt punctuated each of his slowing heartbeats.

"Is there a spell or something you can do to stop this?" I asked Maryanne, hoping she could help the dying detective in some way.

"Rick, I can't. There're too many people around. And he's a detective?! We really don't need this kind of heat right now." She was right. We looked at each other and sighed; the fat man's fate seemed sealed.

"He's lost a lot of blood — he won't make it before 911 gets here." I kept pushing the towels against his weeping wounds when he made a gurgling noise, like he was trying to speak.

"Don't try to talk, Detective Lee," I said in my calmest voice. "Just hang on. Help is on the way. I need you to hold on, Lee."

As I said it, though, I realized there wasn't any help on the way. No one had called. It was just us.

There was movement in the dark corner and Paul nodded his head to draw my attention to Lazarus rising from his seat.

"Watch out, Lazarus coming your way," Paul said while keeping the old woman pinned down. Lazarus stopped beside me and stared as I tried to keep the fat man alive. He stood still, and watched.

Thanks for being so Goddamn helpful, Lazarus.

"I can help him," Lazarus offered after a moment of watching me struggle. "Christo told me how to save him." Lazarus reached forward and placed his hands on either side of the fat man's head; one over his face, one covering the back of his head.

"Lazarus, what are you doing? Stop — that's not helpful!" I shouted.

"I was told how to save him," he said flatly as he rotated his hands so they were on either side of the fat man's face. Then, Lazarus started to pull. Detective's Lee's silent scream turned to a grimace as Lazarus lifted him off the ground by his ears.

"Lazarus, no! Stop! He doesn't need your fucking help!"

There was a series of pops, followed by a ripping sound. Then a dull thud. The fat man's body slumped to the floor as Lazarus stood still, holding the man's head in his hands. There was a stream of blood flowing from what was formerly Detective Lee's throat, pooling around Lazarus's shoes. He stared into the head's eyes. Then he squeezed his hands and with a climactic grunt, the head crumpled between his hands. I could hear the bones crunch as they pierced the brain, and a tiny gust as the air rushed out of the nasal cavity. Lazarus let the barely identifiable mass fall to the floor, where it landed in a pool of blood with a splat.

"Christo says he doesn't want you, or anyone, to interfere with his plans," Lazarus said flatly. He turned to Paul, who still had the old woman pinned down. She was flailing to wrest him off of her but it was no use as Paul was stronger than any of us.

"I can fix this," he said to Paul. "I'll handle this old bitch."

"Oh, will you?!" Paul shouted. "The same way you handled the detective? Because I'm pretty sure you just did more of Christo's dirty work, you asshole. I just watched you rip that guy's head clean off for no good fucking reason!"

Lazarus remained stony-faced. "It had to be done," he said. "Orders must be followed. I am commanded by him. He is my creator."

Lazarus looked at the old woman twisting and turning on the floor, and before Paul could do anything, Lazarus stomped on the side of her head, crushing it immediately. But he continued to stomp on the skull. Over and over again. Paul's face and shirt now drenched with her blood.

Which left us with two headless corpses. Lazarus had murdered them, but Christo was the killer. Paul got up from the floor to stand face to face with Lazarus and looked directly into his eyes.

"I'm getting really fucking tired of the two of you trying to screw things up for me and my friends. Now it stops. All of your bullshit stops NOW!" Paul's voice was deeper than usual, and he sounded extremely angry.

Lazarus blinked twice then said, "I told you, I am only doing what must be done. Now we must go. Do not interfere again. This is your only warning." Then, he left. Walked right out the front door.

I was in shock and could barely move. Maryanne managed to grab onto Paul to catch herself from slipping in the still-pooling blood as she stepped to avoid each of the corpses.

"What happens now?" she asked, her voice unsure.

"Nothing." A faint voice from the back of the café.

…Christo…

Christo got up from his table slowly to approach Maryanne and Paul. "You will not do a damn thing. Otherwise, I'll kill all four of you. And whoever else I please. Do not test me. Do you understand? I can't be stopped, so just stay out of my way, fuckers."

Four? Me. Paul. Maryanne… There's only three of us here.

Then I realized who he meant, who the fourth person was: Lizzie.

"I should end you right here and now, Christo," Paul said, clenching his fists and standing his ground.

"You can try, but you and your witch whore would be the ones being ended. And this pathetic human pet of yours, too,"

Christo said, looking at me. "I am done with your meddling. Have fun cleaning up — you should probably get to it." He frowned at the bodies on the floor before sneering, "I'll catch you all later. Literally." He guffawed as he left. The three of us were left standing in the wake of Christo's destruction.

"What do we do?" Maryanne asked after a moment.

We stood in silence for a moment just looking around and trying to breathe through our mouths. Paul spoke up after what seemed like an eternity. "I think that it's time for a change — A transformation. Tonight, I hunt. Tomorrow, I will end Christo Daggen."

Chapter Fourteen

The night sky was dotted with clouds, and the air was cool and damp. I could sense moisture in the little bit of the fresh air I was able to take in from the half-inch crack in the window on my right; it felt crisp and fresh. The full moon was blood-red and appeared larger than usual, as its light made the stars seem dim in comparison. A red moon was rare — I'd never seen it — but I thought better than to pepper Maryanne and Paul with questions about astronomy.

We'd been driving for almost an hour, all of us jam-packed into Paul's car, leaving me almost no space in which to maneuver. I wanted to stretch my legs or my arms, but was uncomfortably pinned between the corpses and Dead Laura. My extremities were tingling in pain, but at least I wasn't dead like my seatmates, so I kept my complaints to myself.

Loading the backseat would have been funny if it weren't so disgusting. I felt like some tiny plastic toy that some unseen hand was trying to shove in the car; after grunts and painful contortions I squished myself between Dead Laura, and the headless corpses Christo had left us.

I had no idea where the hell we were going to end up — probably another dangerous scenario for which I was ill-equipped — but I'd learned to not ask questions.

Paul was driving, his giant hands gripped the cracked leather of his pint-sized car. Maryanne was in the passenger seat enjoying her legroom while I was stuffed in the back, shoulder-to-shoulder with the bodies, and Dead Laura.

So, three corpses, technically.

Dead Laura's dead head lolled forward then rested on my shoulder. She grunted and her dead brown eyes looked up at me. I was inches from the scar on her throat, which was finally beginning to fade. It had been repulsive: thick, bulky, and a deep bluish-purple. But the small, red tear-shaped droplets that dotted the edge of her scar, and even the cut itself, were obscured by the shades of blue and purple of her rotting skin. If I'd been in a better mood, I probably would have thought the colors were beautiful, like an abstract painting.

God, this is disgusting.

Seeing Maryanne resurrect Laura was the closest I'd come to a 'zombie' or 'Lost One', so I was still adjusting. I had been practicing opening my mind to these new experiences but death, and Dead Laura, were undeniably disgusting. No way to sugarcoat it.

Laura: repulsive in life, repulsive in death... Not to mention that now she smells like rotting meat.

I could see small patches and holes of missing skin where her flesh was starting to deteriorate and peel away from her body. Some spots were nothing more than muscles and tendons attached to her bones. The rancid smell seeping from these new holes reminded me of the bags of moldy food and diapers that piled up in front of my apartment complex on trash day. So, unfortunately, I found the smell familiar, however revolting.

"So, what's the plan?" I finally asked Paul. I nudged Dead Laura off my shoulder and leaned closer to the front seat to clarify, "Do we even have a plan?" I worried we had a mission, but no direction on how to defeat the immortal Christo.

"We're going to kill Christo," Paul muttered under his breath. He kept his eyes trained forward as he drove, but it felt like he was lost.

No shit. I'd kill him myself, if I could.

"And how are we going to do that?"

I had never been that far north of the city before and was more terrified of the surrounding woods than I'd expected. Not to mention the blood-red moon that seemed to fill the night sky as it peeked through the trees. There seemed to be nothing but woods and animals this far north.

"We're close, now," Paul sighed as he told me the plan. "When we get there, I'm going to transform. Then, I will feed to build up my strength. So, when tomorrow comes, I plan to be able to rip Christo to motherfucking pieces." He sounded only somewhat confident, but definitely angry. "I have to be away from people when I hunt, though. I don't want any humans around. Besides Maryanne. And you. Maryanne will protect you, so you'll probably be okay. In a perfect world, you would definitely be okay, but in a perfect world, there would also be no Christo."

This world is far from perfect.

An image of a huge wolf mauling me to death popped into my head. I worried about his razor claws tearing through my chest, and parts of my body getting shredded in his massive jaws. I wasn't sure what Paul-as-a-werewolf was capable of, and could only hope he would use his aggression on the right monster rather than his pathetic human tagalong.

The plan to kill Christo seemed too simple; Paul simply had to turn into a wolf and then hunt? Suspiciously simple, even.

I let out a short, mean laugh. "That's all you have to do to kill him? Then why the hell haven't you done it sooner? You could've saved lives, Paul!" I was shouting, furious. I sounded uncharacteristically assertive, but was terrified, and tired of Christo's bullshit. I was furious with Christo, but taking it out on Paul.

"I don't like to change," Paul snapped, showing his teeth and his aggression. "I *hate* the werewolf; he's a jackass who kills for fun. He lives only for the hunt... The thrill of the chase."

Maryanne put her hand on his shoulder and spoke softly. "Easy, killer. Rick is still new to all this, but he's kept all of our secrets so far. You have to give him time to figure everything out." Maryanne's tone was soothing, but I thought her choice of words was ironic: killer. This was the first thing she'd said since we crammed into the car over an hour ago.

"What he meant to say was that he can't always control the wolf during a change," she said. "The necklace helps, but it doesn't give him complete control when the wolf takes over. He's afraid he's going to hurt somebody, so I usually stay with him when he changes. I won't let him hurt anyone, he knows that. He's really just a big lap dog." She squeezed his shoulder affectionately.

Lap dog? Uh, maybe if the dog had rabies and the lap was on fire.

Vampires. Werewolves. Zombies. And now lap dogs. Apparently, anything was possible.

"Sorry, Rick. I wasn't trying to be a dick. But Maryanne's right; I wouldn't be able to live with myself if I hurt someone during a change.... Not again."

Again. I knew better than to ask but I couldn't help be

curious if he'd actually hurt someone before. Paul didn't seem capable of harming someone. Killing a vicious Vampire? Absolutely. Violence against a human? Never.

The woods were thicker and denser than before; the tree branches overlapped and closed off the view of the sky completely. We passed a single deer on the side of the road that disappeared in the woods as soon as our headlights caught sight. Dead Laura grunted at it, ready to give chase to a hearty meal. Thankfully, she was confined to the car so couldn't blow our cover, such as it was.

The car began to slow and we came to almost a complete stop, deep in the heart of the woods.

The middle of nowhere. Literally. I hope I don't die out here — no one would ever find my body this far north of the city. They wouldn't even know where to begin to look.

"I'll park the car just inside this copse — no one will see us while we're here," Paul said as he eased the car down a well-trodden pathway. He shifted into park about thirty feet into the woods, behind three giant trees. We were surrounded by the wooden giants, and short, dense bushes covered most of the ground. The long shadows and strange forms would make it almost impossible for anyone looking for us to distinguish our bodies from the surrounding woods.

I had a feeling Paul visited those woods frequently to change; he seemed entirely unfazed by the dark surroundings, and had made it very clear that he had to be secluded from the rest of the world during his transformations.

"Rick, mind helping me take care of the bodies while Paul's hunting?" Maryanne asked. She knew I wouldn't tell her no.

Playing with more damn dead bodies... I'm about ready

for Rick's Adventures with Dead Things to come to an end.

"Yeah, sure," I mumbled. "But it's so dark. How are we supposed to see what we're doing when we can't see three feet in front of us? What if a bear sneaks up, or something?" I knew Paul and Maryanne could fend for themselves, but I was feeling shaky.

The only visible light was from Paul's car. I could barely make out the edges of the giant trees that surrounded us. It felt like staring into a black hole of nothing.

"You won't have to worry about that. I'm about to be the scariest thing in these woods. That's for damn sure." Paul opened his door and stepped into the darkness. He pulled his jacket off his shoulders and let it drop to the ground just before he disappeared into the woods.

"You don't need to be afraid of the dark, Rick," Maryanne soothed. "I can fix that once we have a plan, and Paul begins to change." She clearly had something up her sleeve. A witch, a werewolf, and me; I was feeling particularly unremarkable. I still had no clue, why they'd want me there, and was nervous as hell to find out.

Maryanne stepped from the car and motioned for me to follow. And, against my better judgment, I did. At the very least I was desperate to get away from Dead Laura's smell. Once freed from the stinking car, I spun around slowly to take in my surroundings. I was practically enveloped in darkness — there was nothing to cut through the deep shadows of the woods.

I only stopped spinning when I heard a loud rustle somewhere behind me. I couldn't pinpoint where it had come from in the pitch-black woods. I took a steadying breath, but gasped when the noise came again, much louder and much closer. It was like it was in front of me now, charging.

Fast. Very fast. Leaves, sticks, rocks, and earth were crushed with its every step. Whatever it was, it was pulverizing anything it ran across, and I was afraid I was going to be next.

Oh, God. This is it. How I meet my end.

My heart was racing but I was frozen in fear; I couldn't move a muscle. "Maryanne? Paul?!" I cried into the darkness. I wanted someone to come to my rescue. Anyone. Maryanne was nearby but she didn't answer. The sound of breaking branches was getting louder, and closer. Whatever it was I could feel how much it wanted me, and that I didn't stand a chance.

Maryanne startled me when she suddenly appeared and lightly squeezed my arm. "Breathe. You're all right. Everything is fine." She was using soothing tones, but I was frantic and wanted to run. Every instinct in my body was telling me to get the hell out of there.

"But those noises… There's something in the woods, and it's headed straight for us," I whispered, still frozen in fear.

Move, Rick. Turn around and run, you moron!

Maryanne kept her hand on my arm as we heard the noises get closer, and louder. Whatever it was, it had nearly reached us.

Only God can help us now!

I had never been a religious person. But with what I had recently learned of vampires and other supernatural beings, I called out, because maybe there was a God, and maybe he or she would save my life.

"Rick, stay calm. Those noises?" Maryanne gestured to the woods, "You don't have to worry about them. That's just our guest," she said casually. "Who, from the sounds of it, is almost here."

I don't want any guests. I want to leave. Take me back to the car.

The sounds reached an almost deafening climax, and then abruptly stopped. Now the darkness was cloaked in silence, and I wasn't sure which was more terrifying; the noises, or their sudden absence.

I could make out the outlines of a shadowy figure stepping out from behind a tree a few feet in front of me.

"Hey handsome." A familiar voice rose from the woods.

It can't be... Lizzie?

Last I'd seen her, she was exiting the bloody cafe earlier that morning. "Yep. It's me." Lizzie stepped out of the woods and into the little bit of light cast by the still running car. She was wearing what looked like a blue jogging suit. The bottom of her belly ring glinted from the little bit of skin between the zip-up sweatshirt and the waist of her sweatpants. Her hair was in a ponytail. I thought she looked absolutely stunning, and relief flooded me immediately. My fear faded with the sound of her voice.

"I've missed you all day," she said. She kissed my cheek and my whole body felt warm the moment her lips touched my skin. Her touch soothed me.

"Where did you come from?" I asked, amazed. "How did you know where to find us out here?"

"Well, Maryanne told me where Paul would probably be hunting tonight. Plus, I could smell you," Lizzie answered. "By the way, Maryanne, thank you for inviting me out here. I really appreciate it." Lizzie reached for my hand and held it in her firm grip; she was claiming her territory and I never wanted her to let go. Maryanne saw Lizzie take my hand and quickly averted her gaze.

"Also, thanks for covering for me this morning at the café with the detective," Lizzie went on. "You and Paul have been nothing but kind to me. If there's ever anything I can do for either of you, let me know. Anything. This morning really didn't end well, but it could have been a lot worse. Christo could've done a lot more damage. Believe me."

How? If Lizzie was concerned, then I figured there was no chance of me surviving a showdown with Christo that I couldn't seem to escape.

Maryanne smiled at Lizzie. "It's no problem. Of course we need you here because you're going to help us kill him. Plus, I figured Rick would really enjoy your company. Do you need to hunt while we're out here?" Maryanne asked. "You'll need your strength if we're going up against Christo tomorrow."

I wasn't convinced the plan would work, but was sure I didn't want any part of it. Were we just going to surprise him and attack him in the café? What was I supposed to do? I was weak, and a human — no match for an immortal being.

"I'll probably feed on the way home, but what are we doing out here right now?" Lizzie asked Maryanne. "I know that Paul needs to hunt, but what are we doing? And where is Paul anyway?" He had been gone since the time we arrived.

Maryanne waved her hand in dismissal. "He probably just went to grab a bite before he goes through his change. It takes a lot out of him so he needs to eat. I'm sure he'll be back any minute." Maryanne then pointed to the backseat of the car. "But we need to deal with these bodies; we have to get rid of the people Lazarus killed so there aren't any follow-up questions."

Fingers crossed we're dumping Dead Laura, too.

"Whatever you need, I'm here. Just let me know," Lizzie said. She offered her assistance out of duty, and friendship.

"I'm gonna get Dead Laura out of the car. She's probably getting hungry again. I swear that girl's stomach is a bottomless pit. If you and Rick grab the two bodies out of the back, we can get to burying them," Maryanne ordered in a way that didn't sound like a demand. She was always very pleasant and never asked for too much, but was also clearly a master negotiator.

I nodded and turned to head back to the car, less than ten yards from me, but before I could take two steps, Lizzie dropped the bodies at my feet. They were still swaddled in makeshift body bags, but it was horribly clear they were both missing their heads.

"You haven't buried those headless corpses yet?" a deep voice asked from the trees behind us.

I turned around to see Paul step out from the woods. Even in the low light I could see he was wearing nothing except his jeans and sapphire necklace. He was holding the head of a bear as blood dripped out of each side of his mouth, trickling down onto his chest.

"You should see the other guy," he said with a smile. He lifted the bear head high above his head.

Did he really just kill a bear? That's insane... impressive... insane.

"You picked a fight with a bear? And won?" I asked.

I can barely fend off a damn mosquito. Wow.

Paul shrugged. "Wasn't much of a fight after I ripped it's throat out with my teeth." He smiled to bare his teeth, stained crimson-red from what I assumed was the bear's blood.

"Wasn't much the poor beast could do once I got under him and his throat was in my mouth. Nothing to it," Paul chuckled. "The hardest part was ripping the head off."

Yikes.

"I brought Dead Laura a gift," he said as he tossed the bear's head at our feet. "She'll love it."

I'm sure she will.

"Nicely done," Lizzie said, congratulating Paul. "Give us a hand with these bodies?" she asked, giving one of the bags a soft kick. I hoped it was the old woman in that crinkling bag and not the poor detective because she certainly deserved it, and much more than just a kick.

"No," Paul said. "I've got something else I have to do."

"What else do you have to do?" I asked.

He got down on his knees and looked up at us. "It's time for me to become the wolf," he said. He tipped his head toward the blood-red moon, which was almost completely invisible through the trees. "It's time to bring out the animal."

Maryanne led Dead Laura on a metal chain leash to next to the car where she tethered the zombie just feet from the bear's head. Dead Laura sniffed it a few times and then tore into one of the ears, ripping it clean off. The sound of the bear's tearing flesh sent chills down my spine. Blood splattered from the head and landed on my left cheek. Lizzie turned to me in that same moment, licking her lips, and then ran her tongue along my cheek, licking me clean. "Yummy," she whispered in my ear, which I found intensely alluring.

Maryanne stepped towards Paul and fell to her knees, her eyes level with his. She raised her arms high above her head and formed a triangle by touching her thumbs and pointer fingers together, palms up. A single bolt of lightning struck her hands, but she didn't flinch. "Illuminati!" she shouted. She held her arms high above her head and waved them back and forth.

"Illuminati!" she shouted again. The tops of the trees parted to reveal the blood-red moon, which bathed the wooded area in a crimson glow.

God, what the hell. More craziness. Yet again, I had no idea of what was happening around me.

"Will the moonlight hurt you? It's really bright," I said to Lizzie.

"No, we're creatures of the night. Moonlight can't harm us, it doesn't matter how bright it is," she answered, her face illuminated in the red moonglow. "But it's nice of you to be so worried about me," she smiled. She gently rubbed my back, and I felt calmed by her touch.

"Okay, Paul, I'm here and I'm not going anywhere. Get to shifting." Maryanne stood and backed up a little while yelling to Lizzie and me over her shoulder, "You two should back up. Give him some room."

Absolutely. You know best.

Lizzie and I took a few steps back and my uneasiness grew. Something was about to happen and it was making me nervous.

"Is this normal?" I asked Maryanne as we stepped back. "And what's with the moon? Is this all right?" All questions I should have asked a long time ago but my nerves were getting the best of me.

"It's fine, Rick. And that?" She looked briefly up at the moon. "It's a supermoon, and it can power up a werewolf for twenty-four hours. It is a rare occurrence, but the power it gives is unmatched. Nothing stronger. Not even Christo."

"What?" Lizzie asked. "I've never heard of any of this."

"We all keep secrets," Maryanne answered. "Surely you can understand that."

Paul was still on his knees, shirtless. He roared, clenched his right hand into a tight fist, and repeatedly punched the ground, sending dirt and pebbles into the air with every blow. Sweat was pouring down his back as he struck at the earth. He tipped his head towards the moon and howled in pain, like a lone wolf searching for his pack. In between landing punches, I saw the skin on his right hand start to crack, like small rips in his skin.

Blood dripped as the cracks widened — he was shedding his human skin. He continued to howl.

I could barely believe what I was seeing.

Paul's human hand had been replaced with an extremity covered in thick black fur, his fingernails replaced with razor-sharp claws. His body was changing piece by piece. His right arm was no longer human, and the sheded skin landed in a pile on the ground beneath him. It was steaming.

Paul lifted his werewolf arm and claws to his face. Starting at his forehead, he sunk his sharp werewolf claws deep into his skin. He howled as he ripped the human skin off of his face. The man I knew as 'Paul' was disappearing in front of me, and he was becoming a monster of many myths. A legend.

I could see patches of black fur poking through where the skin had been torn. His face was gushing with blood as his nose extended into a long, thick snout. His teeth had turned into immense fangs. The remnants of Paul's human face fell to the ground in pieces. His head was now a complete wolf's head, but much larger than any wolf I'd ever seen.

He hunched forward and put his snout to the pile of human skin on the ground. He opened up his werewolf maw and began eating his human skin, devouring himself. I could see his human face being ripped to shreds between his massive jaws.

Once he'd finished, the creature stood up and revealed its full height; he had to be nearly seven feet tall. Fucking huge. I stood in fear and awe in front of the werewolf. Maryanne was standing calmly, but I gripped Lizzie's hand as tightly as I could as my heart pounded.

"He's not going to hurt us," Lizzie offered in reassurance. "It's all right, Rick." But she had never been around him during his change, so who was to say what he was going to do? Paul had been right, though, as he was absolutely the scariest thing in those woods that night. Probably any night.

The wolfman then sunk his claws deep into the top of his left shoulder near the edge of his human skin and howled as the claws pierced flesh. He peeled the human skin from his left arm and his chest, and it came off in one large sheet of steaming epidermis. It was soaked in blood and sweat, but Paul was now a wolfman from the waist up. His jeans were still on and intact, but his boots hadn't survived the change because Paul's feet had grown, too. The claws poked through the toes of the boots, then his feet swelled and burst through them so the boots lay in small shreds of leather around him. The feet were covered in the same heavy, black fur that masked his head and torso. He was a giant furry beast. All that was left was his jeans, and whatever human parts were beneath them.

With another howl, he pushed his sharp claws through the denim and straight into his hip. Blood immediately poured from the punctures, staining his blue jeans red. The claws shredded down the sides of his legs, tearing his flesh and denim all the way to his feet. I could hear the skin and denim ripping. With one smooth motion the werewolf raised his arms above his head so the rest of his human skin sloughed off to the ground beneath him.

Paul was no longer himself. He had completed the transition and now we were met with a seven-foot wolfman. A werewolf. I had an impulse to reach out, to touch him just to make sure he was real, but my better sense prevailed.

In that moment I wanted to run, and to leave all the craziness behind. But what about... her? Lizzie. There was no way in hell I would leave her. I had never felt this way about anything, let alone anyone. The closest I'd ever been to falling in love was probably with a bottle of gin. I couldn't say whether I was falling in love with Lizzie, but something new was happening and it was making me feel things I'd never felt before.

Maryanne turned away from the wolfman and came back over to Lizzie and me. "Rick, Lizzie. I'd like you both to meet Triton. The werewolf inside of Paul," she said in a quiet tone.

Triton? It has a name? I wasn't sure of the proper way to address him, and even Lizzie looked a little confused.

"Hello, Rick." A deep voice came from the werewolf. From Triton.

"Are you okay?" I asked a little hysterically, given the transformation we'd just witnessed.

"I'm better than ever. And I know you two are friends, I feel everything that Paul feels," the werewolf said. "After all, I am his better and stronger half. But even Paul doesn't know how to feel about her," Triton pointed at Lizzie as he stepped forward. "The vampire."

I instinctively stood in front of Lizzie. I was no match for a werewolf, especially Triton, but still I managed to say, "Lizzie is a friend, too."

"Vampires are not good company, Rick." The deep-voiced Triton stepped closer, not taking his eyes off of Lizzie.

"This one is, Triton," Maryanne said, darting to put herself between the werewolf and the two of us. "You know you can trust me. Lizzie is a friend. She's going to help us kill Christo."

The werewolf stood silent, then lowered his claws as he took a couple steps back. "Hrrrrm. Just be sure this vampire is on the right side tomorrow. Paul hates Christo with a passion. He wants him to burn."

Get in line, man.

"I'm hungry." Triton sniffed the air. "Maryanne, take them back and I'll meet you at the café before morning."

"Okay, we'll head back as soon as we're done here," Maryanne said, gesturing to the still-topside corpses.

In that same second, Lizzie dropped my hand and was gone. So were the bodies. Three seconds later, she was back at my side, her face marked with little bits of dirt on each of her cheeks underneath her eyes. "It's done. The bodies are buried," she said, smiling.

She's so fast.

"Thanks," Maryanne said. "That helps a lot. Now we can get outta here."

Triton sniffed again, announced, "I'm going to eat," then was gone.

I felt much safer without the werewolf around. Though I hoped he'd be able to build up enough strength to destroy Christo, I still found his presence unsettling. "Can we please get the fuck out of here?" I pleaded.

Lizzie walked up behind me and wrapped her arms around my torso. She rested her head on my shoulder. "I'll get him home, Maryanne, if that's all right?" Lizzie asked.

"Yeah, of course. I'm just going to get Dead Laura back to Paul's basement, and figure out what spells will work the best on Christo." Maryanne untied Dead Laura's leash from the tree and called out, "I'll see you two later on."

Maryanne stuffed Dead Laura into the back of Paul's car and then got into the driver's seat. I watched as the car reversed down the path, and then the headlights quickly disappeared in the thick woods. Pretty soon I wasn't able to see my hand in front of my face because it was so dark. The trees resumed their usual posture as Maryanne left, which completely blocked the supermoon's light, and we were once again enveloped by the night.

I felt a hand on my neck and prayed to God it was Lizzie. She moved her hand slowly down the front of my chest and made her way to the zipper on my jeans. I could feel myself thickening as her fingers danced across my lap. Lizzie then unzipped my jeans completely and grabbed my stiffening cock. She tugged gently and my whole body tingled. She moved her hand up and down my shaft slowly as she began to gently kiss the back of my neck. She moved her mouth up and carefully bit the base of my ear, instilling the perfect amount of pain. She licked the skin behind my ear and then whispered, "Are you ready for me, handsome?"

Chapter Fifteen

Triton charged and thrashed his way through the woods in search of something else to eat. He tore through leaves and branches with his razorblade claws and his gigantic werewolf feet crushed the earth, leaving an aggressively-beaten path in his wake.

His system was flooded with an infusion of energy and strength from the blood of the bear he'd just killed, but Triton needed more. He knew he would need as much strength as he could get if he wanted to stand a chance against Christo.

He sensed something close — something fresh. Whatever it was, he could smell that it was barely alive, if at all. He followed the scent.

After what seemed like hours of crashing through the woods, Triton came upon a campfire that had almost completely burned out. He knelt and held his fur-covered hand over the center of the circle of stones, and immediately felt the heat from the still glowing embers. The heat was intense but Triton could withstand immense amounts of heat, cold, and pain — perhaps more than any other creature in the supernatural world.

Triton turned and saw two tents pitched around the makeshift fire pit. Articles of clothing and empty green beer bottles were scattered around the area; shirts, hats, socks, Heineken. He inhaled deeply to capture every scent around him which further inflamed his killer senses. He was in the middle of someone's campsite, and he knew that if the campers reappeared, he would viciously tear them apart, whoever they were. Limb by limb, bite by bite, he would end them.

The werewolf picked up a red woven scarf and put it to his snout. His heightened olfactory senses immediately identified the scent: woman. His eyes dilated as her smell filled his nose, and his mouth watered as he imagined her intestines unspooling between his teeth. He desperately wanted to taste her insides — to feel her warm blood hit his face as he gashed her stomach open with his massive claws.

The logical, human side of Triton knew he had to leave the campsite before anyone returned or else they'd be dead. He tossed the red scarf back to the ground, but the woman's scent lingered in his nostrils. He slipped out of the clearing to return to tearing through the woods at top speed. Felled trees and splintered boughs lay in his wake of destruction. But the scent invigorated the werewolf, and whatever remaining control Paul had over Triton was waning fast; he couldn't control himself, or his urge to gut the scarf's owner.

He only stopped running when he came to the edge of a cliff. He could hear the rush of a stream below, and his snout caught lingering traces of the woman. His werewolf senses transcended biology, so even the rushing water could not mask the scent; Triton's lust for the taste of the woman's insides was primordial.

Without hesitation, Triton leaned forward and launched himself over the edge of the cliff. He roared as he hit the water. The rushing water reached almost to his massive shoulders, but he pressed forward, determined to find his quarry. The scent was stronger and more intoxicating — he knew he had to be close. He could almost taste her.

Triton flipped heavy rocks and downed tree limbs from under the water to find the scent's source. He thrashed against the upstream flow until he was almost completely submerged, his snarling head just visible above the water. He began to tire as he fought the intensifying current from the now raging river. He roared as he pushed through the rapids, still searching for her. He'd never had such a hard time landing his prey.

Triton finally heaved his soaked body onto the shore where he laid on his back, panting. The werewolf had worn himself out fighting the rapids, but the scent continued to taunt him; he felt she had to be close. His snout still tingled from her fragrance, and his cravings were beyond control. He had to have her. A mixture of river water and bile splattered on the shore as Triton rolled over to cough up the water from his lungs. His eyes were shut tight as he retched so it took a moment to notice what was laying on the shore.

A middle-aged woman with brown hair was lying dead beside him. She had on a pair of blue jeans and, from what Triton could tell, what had once been a red and white striped t-shirt. Even on that water-logged ground he could see a pool of blood surrounding the body, streaming from multiple punctures in the neck. Her chest had been ripped open, revealing her sternum. Organs and flesh spilled from the body and Triton was faced with a grisly scene that he had not created, though it had been his intent. As much as he'd wanted to shred the body and gobble it up, he was evidently not the first monster to reach the woman, which made his stomach turn, because he had a good idea of who could have managed this carnage: Christo.

The werewolf stood up and looked at the body. Carnage

aside, he still wanted to eat her. He was fatigued from battling the river, and the woman's guts were calling out to him. Triton knew that those glistening human parts, plus the bear from earlier might give him enough energy to take down Christo.

Triton shoved the blade extending from his index finger deep into the body's chest cavity. He gathered the organs in his hand and twisted his wrist so the intestines wrapped around his fingers, then pulled everything from the inside out. He brought the bloody contents to his mouth and began to chew on the parts. He chewed through flesh and tendons, and felt the organs pop and gush inside his mouth. Was that a kidney? Or maybe the liver? He didn't care what — it was delicious. The barely-warm blood stained his gums and teeth. Triton was satisfied, but for the heart; his belly was gurgling, and he knew that the heart provided the most energy.

The woman's body was basically an empty shell, as the heart was the only thing left after Triton had pulled out her insides. Again, he reached deep inside the chest where he could feel that the heart was still attached. He sliced the organ free with his claws, ripped it out and held it above his head. He tipped his head back, opened his gleaming jaws, and squeezed the heart as hard as he could. The blood spurted from the severed aorta into his mouth and dripped down the back of his throat. Once drained, Triton ripped the heart in two and tossed one half into his mouth. He chewed and chewed, pulverizing the organ with his sharp teeth and caustic saliva so that he could take in every bit of her essence. He could feel the spirit of the woman flowing through his veins. He swallowed eagerly and then ate the rest.

With each bite he could feel himself getting stronger — he felt invincible.

Triton finished eating, but felt a pang of emotion for the nameless, lifeless woman. She didn't deserve Christo's wrath — no one did — but hoped that her sacrifice would be enough to take down the sadistic son-of-a-bitch. The werewolf picked up the shell of a body and carried it to the base of a nearby weeping willow. He gently placed it by the trunk and began to cover it with dirt, leaves and bits of brush. Soon, the body was completely covered, and Triton was left to hunt. But his target was neither man, nor beast; he was pursuing a thousand-year-old killing machine. He was chasing Christo.

Chapter Sixteen

It was pitch black and I couldn't see a thing. The night air was cool and crisp against my skin, and the red light of the moon was obscured completely by the thick trees. Lizzie and I were alone. I couldn't see her but I could feel her, smell her, and sense her. I could smell a soft vanilla scent surrounding her body, leaving me almost intoxicated. I couldn't stop breathing her in.

She stood behind me and gently rubbed my shoulders, urging me to relax. The front of my pants were undone, and I wanted her to massage in between my legs. I craved her touch again.

She kissed my neck and a tingle shot through my entire body. I was a little concerned given how interested she'd been in my neck a few nights prior, but the part of me that was worried was no competition for the part of me that wasn't. Her touch felt so good that I didn't want her to stop caressing me. She ran her fingers through my hair. I wanted her, and felt determined to be with her again, to be inside her warmth.

Lizzie licked my earlobe and I closed my eyes. In the pitch black I pictured what she looked like pressed against me and tried to lean into the moment, no matter how strange and new the experience. I had only been with one woman — her — and just the one time, so I felt like I was still finding my sea legs.

"Are you ready for me, handsome?" she whispered in my

ear again, giving it another small nibble.

You have no idea how ready I am.

"I think I have some idea," she responded to my thought. She ran her hand down my front and then squeezed my thickening cock. I blinked and suddenly she was in front of me, holding me close in an embrace. She wrapped her arms around me, and held me tight. I flung my arms around her to hold her, too. I couldn't see anything but I didn't need to; I knew exactly what I wanted to do with her.

I felt her fingers tilt my head to hers and her lips locked onto mine, her mouth open against mine. Her tongue slipped into my mouth and sparred and tangled with my own as we pressed against each other more urgently. I'd never been kissed like that before.

I remembered what it felt like to be inside her; warm, wet, and so damned tight. I wanted my cock surrounded by her gorgeous perfection again. I wanted her just as she was; I wouldn't change a single thing about her. Not even the bloodsucking.

Lizzie pulled her tongue from my mouth for just a second. "I'm going to lay you down on the ground, okay?" She lightly pushed my chest and gently laid me back, cradling the back of my head. I couldn't see, but I trusted her with every part of me. I trusted her with my life and felt safe that she would never let anything bad happen to me.

Once on the ground, she immediately started kissing me again. I felt her carefully mount my lap so her legs were straddling my thighs. She moved her mouth to my neck. I opened my eyes but could barely see the red moon through the thick layers of trees above us. Even in the eerie, dark clearing in the woods I felt like I was in the middle of my very own fairytale.

Lizzie's hands ran across my chest before she swiftly pulled my shirt up and over my head. She caressed the bare skin of my chest, pinched my tiny nipples, then started to work her way to my waist. I could feel myself getting even harder.

"Do you want me, Rick?" she whispered in my ear as she reached inside of my boxers and tugged on me firmly.

"I want you forever and always." The words slipped from my lips before I even realized what I was saying. I leaned into her to kiss her neck when she freed my erect cock from my boxers and began to slide her hand up and down. Her grip was exhilarating.

"I was hoping you'd say that," she whispered as I heard the zipper of her top slowly come undone. I reached forward, groping for her breasts in the darkness, and they were right in front of me. I ran my hands under her tits to feel their heft and then gently squeezed. She moaned next to my ear; I felt that I had to be doing something right, and I wanted more.

I ran my hands down the sides of her ribcage and was amazed by how soft her smooth skin felt under my rough hands. I reached for her tight ass. I found the waistband of her sweatpants and slowly pushed them down past her hips and thickly-rounded bottom. I was surprised, then thrilled to find she wasn't wearing panties.

Lizzie continued rubbing my cock, and then suddenly pulled my pants and boxers down to my feet in one motion. We were completely naked on the forest floor, her on top of me like some nymph goddess. A fleeting thought of small rocks and pebbles ending up where they shouldn't, crossed my mind, but I was willing to take the risk for her.

"I want you to feel what you do to me," she said to me

seductively. She took my left hand and put it between her legs. She pushed my fingers up against her smoothly shaven slit, and I could feel how wet she was.

Oh, my god. She is so fucking hot…

I gently pushed two of my fingers deep into her womanhood and was again amazed by how tight she was. I slid them out a little and then forced them back in. In and out. Repeatedly, and each time my fingers became more slick, more wet. I tickled her pussy and then all I could think of was my cock inside of her, and I hoped she wanted the same thing.

Should I ask her if I can put it in now?

"Yes. Yes. Put it in me now." She was still moaning as she read my mind again.

"Oh, thank God," I answered, both relieved and thrilled. It was so dark I couldn't see her on top of me and worried my dick would somehow get lost on its way to her waist. But Lizzie moved her hips forward to meet mine and the next thing I knew our groins met, and I was in ecstasy. I was deep inside her and I never wanted to leave.

She rode me, bouncing up and down so my member slipped in and out of her glistening vagina. I laid back in the darkness and enjoyed her enjoying the ride.

"I want you to bite me. Please don't drink too much this time." The words came out of my mouth before I could fully appreciate what I was asking her to do. Again.

"No," she snapped. She was still moving her hips up and down on my shaft. She'd been clear in her response but I couldn't focus on anything but her body, and how it fit with mine like mated pieces of a puzzle.

"I want you to bite me," I said forcefully. "Please."

She pushed her hips down on my cock as far as she could,

and I thought I was going to explode right then. It was taking all my concentration not to come yet, so I wrapped my arms around her lower back to pull her hips even closer to me. I wanted to be as deep inside her as physically possible. She winced and we grunted in unison when our pelvises smashed into each other.

"I will bite you, but under one condition," she whispered in my ear. "Drink my blood again. I want you to have me in your system when we go up against Christo. For protection. I can't lose you — you are everything." Lizzie rode me harder and I never wanted to let her go. I wanted to hold her forever.

"All right, I will drink from you. After you bite me. I want to feel that connection again. Being with you is… incredible. Honestly. But when you bit me, it was even more intense. I've never felt anything like it… I never felt anything until I met you." We had reached the terms and I was more focused than ever on her biting my neck. It defied logic, but I needed her fangs in me.

Lizzie started kissing my neck again, and I was ready and nervous. She pushed her face deeper into the curve from my jaw to my neck and I could feel the tips of her teeth beginning to brush against me, barely enough to graze my skin. With a sharp inhale, she pushed her head forward and I felt her pierce me, her fangs plunging deep into my soft neck. I could feel my blood as she sucked on my neck, coaxing bits of my essence, my lifeforce. Whatever pain I'd felt from the initial bite gave way to a light-headed euphoria brought on by the intense connection I felt with her, and the massive blood loss.

She kept riding me with her hips as she sucked on my neck, and I hoped she could control herself. She pulled her head up and away from me and, even in the darkness, I could see my blood glinting from her mouth. She licked her lips, smiled at me, then went back to my neck again.

Careful.

My body spasmed when she bit me again, but all I could focus on was the intense pleasure. "Make me cum, angel. Make me cum now," I begged her as the blood loss left me barely conscious. Even in the moment I found it funny that I would call this demon an angel.

She bucked against me with all her might and my naked ass bounced against the ground. She thrust three, four times before she sat herself fully on my cock, pulling all of me inside her. I saw stars, my eyes rolled, and I erupted inside of her like a volcano. The moment I came, she pulled her fangs out of my neck and I had never felt so good in my entire life. Euphoric, and high.

"Are you okay?" she asked. She sounded worried that she had drunk too much from me again.

My neck was sore but I knew her blood would heal my wounds and make me feel like a brand-new man. "I'm fine — just a little light-headed, that's all. I'm great. Really."

Lizzie made a deep cut in her own neck with her fingernail then pulled my head towards her. She forced my mouth over her open wound, which I knew wouldn't be open and bleeding for very long. I suckled the blood from the demon's neck, just as she did from mine. I could feel the holes in my neck start to heal immediately, and my head stopped spinning. The pain in my neck vanished as I nursed at Lizzie's neck, delighting in the sweet and savory taste of her vampire blood.

"Good. Now you should have added protection if we have any issues with that asshole, Christo." Lizzie pulled my mouth away from her throat, which was already healed, like mine now was. "With any luck, everything will be fine. Let's not worry about things we can't control." It had been proven to me time and again that Christo could not be controlled, so I was grateful for her concern, and protection.

How the hell am I going to get home?

I hoped she wasn't going to leave me to fend for myself. Especially since Maryanne had taken the car, and Paul was off being wolfy somewhere — I was doing my best to steer clear of him during his animalistic times.

"I'll get you home," she read my mind again.

"Okay, great," I said with a nervous chuckle. "I was a little worried about how I was going to get out of here. Where will you go tonight?" She'd told me she didn't have a home of her own and I wondered where she spent her time.

"I was hoping I could stay with you tonight?"

Fuck yes. YES.

"I think that would be really nice, Lizzie." I would have let her stay with me every night if she wanted. Even though she didn't sleep, I wanted to sleep next to her, to wake with her. And — selfishly, cowardly — I felt safer having my very own personal vampire to protect me while I slept.

Is that really a safe thing?

We managed to get dressed in total darkness, then Lizzie got behind me and scooped me up like a baby. "So, let's get going," she said. "I'm going to carry you back through the woods and we'll be back to your apartment in just a few minutes. Just hold onto me."

Always and forever. Cradle me, gorgeous — hold me tight. Why is this necessary?

"I'm going to run. Fast. So, seriously, hold on." I wondered if I was ever going to get used to her reading my mind.

I knew I was safe in her arms and that she could protect me from everything, anything… Except him. Nobody could keep me safe from him. I'd known Christo for years and had always kept my distance. But once Lizzie started coming around and Pandora's box-of-supernatural-things had been opened, I smartened up and knew to be deathly afraid of him and what he was capable of. Just like in poker; better to know when you're outmatched than to throw it all away on a bad call. Know your enemies, and know your limitations.

Lizzie acted like holding me took no effort at all — like I weighed no more than a small sack of potatoes. She never ceased to amaze me. I was in awe, but also painfully jealous that everything was so easy for her.

My vampire queen darted through the woods while she held me close. Trees and bushes became a blur as we zipped past them with her incredible speed. I tried to mark our surroundings to identify where we were, but it was like trying to read a book as someone rapidly turned the pages in front of my face.

I was beginning to feel nauseated so I closed my eyes tight. I didn't want her to think I was scared, but I was, and there was absolutely no hiding it. I could still feel the wind pricking my face, but with my eyes shut at least I wouldn't vomit on her at high speed.

I finally opened my eyes as we exited the woods and were met with a cloudless night sky. The stars winked at me and the moon shone a pinkish-red. I could see we were approaching the city as the New York skyline and its surrounding light pollution drew closer as we hurtled south. We had clearly gone a long way in a very short amount of time.

"How are you doing?" Lizzie asked. She must have been

able to tell that I was extremely unnerved — I wondered if she could feel my body shake. "You holding up all right?" She kept running, and I kept shaking.

"Yeah, I'm fine," I shouted, desperate for her to stop asking.

"We're almost there. We'll have to jump a few rooftops once we get in the city to avoid being seen, okay?" She hugged me closer while still cradling me gently. "It'll be fun," she smiled. "Embrace new experiences. Are you ready?"

"Ready for what?" I didn't know what for, and had a feeling I wasn't even close to being ready. I worried about what was going to come next, but figured it couldn't be worse than trying to suppress nausea while running through the woods at high speed.

"This." Suddenly, Lizzie leapt high into the air. It felt like an airplane taking off. I trusted her, but I also thought I was going to die. I looked up and the stars seemed closer. The moon, too. But I made the mistake of looking down.

The fear of rising too quickly was nothing compared to the fear of falling too fast. The skyscrapers that had seemed so small a few seconds before were growing much larger, very quickly. The ground was getting closer. I was able to make out streetlights, then vehicles, then mailboxes. We were falling, fast. I assumed we were plummeting to our deaths.

"Lizzie! This fall will kill me — It'll kill both of us!" I was shouting over the roar of the air rushing past my ears. She seemed unconcerned.

"Lizzie, please! Do something! I don't want to die — we just started having sex!" Shouting it out loud made me realize how I was really feeling, where my priorities were. The truth was; I didn't want to die because I wanted more time with her. She was the only thing that mattered to me.

"You're not gonna die, Rick. I promise. You drank my blood less than an hour ago, so you should be covered for the next twenty-three hours."

I looked down to see that we were about to land, which scared the shit out of me. The area looked familiar but it was hard to tell from the air. I shut my eyes again as that nauseating feeling was threatening to return. There was a loud thud, and I assumed we had landed.

"We're back on the ground safely," Lizzie reassured me. "I mean, we're not really on the ground. We're on a roof. Your roof."

I looked around; we were indeed on the roof of my building.

Oh, thank God. On land. But how are we supposed to get in now? The roof door is always locked.

"We'll just jump onto the fire escape and go in through your kitchen window. Just like I did the first time I came to see you." Her ability to read my thoughts seemed quaint after our incredible journey and the looming battle with Christo.

I walked over to the roof's edge above the fire escape. Knowing that I was currently just about invincible, I leapt off the edge and landed directly on the metal staircase. I was amazed at my own success. I looked back to see if Lizzie had witnessed my heroic jump, but I didn't see her. I looked down to make sure she hadn't plummeted to her death only to see her sitting on the fire escape stairs, flashing her bright and beautiful smile at me.

"What took you so long?" she said.

"Very funny." I wanted to be like her in so many ways.

"Oh, come on. Let's get inside," she said, pushing me towards my kitchen window. Luckily, I had left it unlocked. I pushed up on the sash and slid the window up. I had never broken into an apartment before. Another first.

I clambered through the open window and turned to offer Lizzie my hand. "You all right? You've done this before, remember?" I smiled at her. She climbed in and I walked straight into my bedroom, hoping she would follow me. We'd had sex in the woods less than an hour ago, but I wanted more of her.

I pulled the covers back and crawled in, grateful for my bed and eager to share it with Lizzie again. "Care to join me?" I asked as I patted the bed next to me.

She stood silently for a beat before saying, "I would love to join you." She climbed into bed beside me but then said, "But you need to sleep, okay? Tomorrow could be very eventful... and dangerous."

After all I'd seen and learned the past weeks, I was terrified of what tomorrow might bring.

Lizzie wrapped her arms around me and kissed my cheek. "Sweet dreams, handsome," she said to me quietly. I closed my eyes and the adrenaline from the day left my body all at once, leaving only exhaustion.

"Will you stay with me while I sleep?" I asked.

"Of course. I'll be right here when you wake up in the morning." Her words floated into my ears as I began to sink into a deep sleep. I'd never slept next to anyone before, but in that half-conscious moment I realized I'd never felt more secure than I did with her next to me.

Lizzie gently stroked my hair as I succumbed to sleep. I closed my eyes to the welcome sight of her lying next to me, caressing me until I fell into a deep sleep.

Chapter Seventeen

When I opened my eyes, Lizzie was still laying in my bed with her arms wrapped around me, holding me tight. I was in the same position as when I'd passed out from exhaustion. Her eyes sparkled as she greeted me, "Good morning, handsome." The sunshine streaming through my window bathed her in a yellow glow that seemed to accentuate every curve of her beautiful body. It was nice waking up to something beautiful.

"You're still here," I croaked, my surprise more than evident.

She's still here. She stayed with me... Waking next to her almost made up for all those years of starting the day alone.

Lizzie released me from her embrace, stretched briefly, then folded her hands over her belly. "I told you I wouldn't leave," she chided gently. "I would never lie to you, Rick."

I didn't have any reason not to trust her; she'd been honest with me about, well, everything. So I resolved to believe her.

"I'm sorry, that's not what I meant to say. I'm really glad you're still here." I hoped she could hear my sincerity. "Really glad." She was the best thing that had ever happened to me, and she deserved to know it.

"Good, me too." She leaned in to kiss her cool lips against my forehead and, though her skin was cold, it was the warmest thing I had ever felt.

Lizzie got up and looked briefly out the window at the

dirty alley that separated my crumbling building from the crumbling building next door. I hated the view, and could tell she was less than impressed. She made a slight frown before turning back to me. "Are you hungry? I could whip up something quick before we head back to the café, if you like." I remembered the first breakfast she made for me: perfectly buttered toast and a glass of orange juice with a few drops of blood mixed in.

"No, I think I'm good. I'll just grab a muffin or something from Maryanne."

Actually, I'd love one of Maryanne's muffins right now…

"I know! They're delicious, aren't they?" Lizzie announced.

Sheesh. Right. That mind reading trick of hers.

I smiled back at her, afraid that she knew I was thinking about Maryanne's 'muffins' and not baked goods. I'd never had a relationship before and wasn't sure if my thoughts were supposed to be strictly monogamous — I'd moved through the world constantly thinking dirty thoughts about multiple women. But things were different with Lizzie — she made me want to be a better person. For myself, and for her.

"Put these on," she said, tossing me a pair of jeans she pulled from the dresser drawer, which I stepped into then zipped up with force. I was admittedly sorry to be obstructing Lizzie's access to my manhood, as sex with her was about all I cared about. There were pressing issues though; Christo now, sexual exploration later.

I was getting anxious about our impending trip to the café. An image of Christo literally tearing me in pieces crossed my mind. I'd not actually considered the level, and type of danger Christo posed to us — me, especially — but his trail of recent killings was making me extremely anxious. He was ruthless in his violence and clearly enjoyed it, so my nerves were working overtime.

"What are we going to do?" I stammered.

Lizzie stared at me for a moment before responding, "What do you mean?" I couldn't tell if she was confused by my question, or if she was shielding me from an ugly truth.

"I mean, what are we going to actually do against Christo? To stop him?" I was starting to sweat. Lizzie walked over to me and put her hand on the back of my head. She gently rested her forehead against mine and looked directly into my eyes. I could see that the very center of her pupils, were bright red, as if a fire was burning inside her skull. I wondered if it was a manifestation of her passion for me? The same burning desire I felt when I looked at her? Or were the flames fanned by her hatred of Christo, or the things he'd done? My mind was racing, but even in my state of panic staring into her eyes made my dick jump.

"Listen to me," she said. "You have my blood in your system, you can't die right now."

...*Right now*... The quantifier brought little relief.

"If something does happen to you, chances are you will become immortal, like me. The chances that you would actually die are small." Very small, I hoped. Her soothing showed me I still had a lot to learn. The one thing I knew for certain was that I never wanted to go back to living in a world without her. She was constantly showing me new experiences for which I would always be grateful. She was the first person to ever take a real interest in me, too. I was still surprised that she wanted me, but that alone made me want her more. I knew that I was lucky I'd gotten to know her and never wanted to let her go.

"Plus, Paul is very, VERY strong. Especially today." She paused, but continued to look into my eyes. "And, Rick — I will literally give my life for you if I have to. I will die making sure you're kept safe. I promise." I believed her, which made me scared for her. No one had ever said anything so meaningful to me before, and I had no way of protecting her. Who was going to keep her safe? I physically shuddered at the thought of losing her after everything we'd been through, after she'd trusted me with her secrets. I wished there was a way for me to help keep her safe.

Feeling useless, and afraid, and vulnerable was too much, and I started to choke up. I could feel my eyes start to water. A single tear — solitary and lonely, like I'd been before I met Lizzie — ran silently down my cheek.

"It's all right, Rick," she said as she wiped the tear away with her thumb. "We are both going to be all right. You'll see." I knew the best thing for me to do was to trust her. It's not like I could face Christo alone. We had to stay and fight.

"God, I hope you're right. I just wish there was more I could do to help you fight him. To help you kill him." I sniffled. "I feel like such a waste of space… Just so damn worthless."

Lizzie pressed her lips to mine then held my face between her hands and said, "You are not worthless, Rick. You are everything to me — the opposite of a waste of space. Truly. I want to be with you, and I mean it." She flashed her gorgeous smile before continuing, in a serious tone, "Now, we really need to get going. We have to meet Paul and Maryanne."

When she mentioned them, I felt a glimmer of hope; we weren't in the fight against Christo alone. I had friends who were determined to bring him down — powerful, supernatural friends — who I hoped would find a way to kill him that didn't end with all of us six feet under.

I looked at my reflection in the mirror, took a steadying breath, and resolved to get prepared for whatever was coming. I adjusted my glasses, tied my shoes, zipped my hoodie, and patted the wallet in my back pocket. I had my vampire queen by my side, and we were ready to go; whatever was coming our way we would face head-on, together.

Just then, there was a knock at the door. Lizzie and I traded a puzzled look. "Were you expecting someone to stop by?" she asked in a low voice as she moved silently toward the door.

"No, not that I know of," I replied, equally curious. "No one 'stops by' to see me." Lizzie had been my first uninvited guest.

She sidled up to the door. She was directly facing it when—

BOOM!

The explosion sent the door sailing across my apartment in two pieces, split perfectly down the middle. One half hit the cupboards across the kitchen, knocking one of the cabinet doors off of its brass hinges. The other half landed atop my kitchen table, shattering the salt shaker and my coffee mug. Absurdly, I was relieved that the coffee cup was empty.

I looked for Lizzie to make sure she wasn't hurt but of course, she was fine. She'd used her incredible vampire speed to get herself out of the way of the explosion and was now standing across the room. She was looking in my direction but past me, at something behind me in the now-shattered entrance. I could tell something was off.

This isn't good.

With some hesitation, I turned toward the open space where my door used to be and there he stood: tall, bald, hulking Lazarus Bedding. He was awkwardly staring at me, his hands at his sides. Even standing in the hallway I could see his front fangs extending over his bottom lip, and the blood dripping from them made me start literally shaking. I'd gotten somewhat comfortable with Lizzie's vampirisms, but Lazarus's fangs terrified me. I thought I was about to die.

"Rick, has Lazarus ever been in your apartment before?" Lizzie asked in a concerned tone. I furrowed my brow trying to remember.

"Umm, uhhh, yeah. But only a few times a long time ago," I stuttered. "Why?" I'd barely gotten the word out when Lazarus cut in.

"I'm sorry, Rick."

You should be sorry, you dickhead lackey.

He was looking at me like I was a creature being stalked, hunted. "I'm here for Christo. He wants you dead. He has compelled me to kill you." Lazarus's voice was deep and quiet, and his words sent shivers up and down my spine.

Christ, what do I do now? He doesn't need to be invited in to get inside... There was nothing I could do to stop him.

"Run, Rick!" Lizzie shouted as she jumped forward, pushed me to the ground, and darted down the hallway in one swift motion. She moved so quickly it looked like she was flying. I heard Lazarus and Lizzie trade snarling growls, like two dogs fighting for dominance.

I looked up and saw Lizzie perched above my head near the ceiling, her hands and feet digging into the wall to hold herself up. Lazarus was still mostly in the hallway, but had stepped closer to the doorframe, completely blocking our escape.

My eyes darted around the room until I saw the kitchen window, still open a crack from when Lizzie and I had climbed through from the fire escape the night before. The fire escape! It seemed like our only shot at getting out alive. I knew that Lizzie was fast and strong, but I wasn't sure she could kill Lazarus by herself, and I wouldn't be much help. We couldn't fight, so we had to leave. Lizzie's safety was my number one priority, and I was hers; I wanted to protect her so that she could protect me, too.

I was still on the ground as I shouted, "The fire escape! We have to get the fuck out of here!" I craned my neck to see Lizzie still clinging to the walls.

"No," she said immediately. "It wouldn't matter. Christo has marked you for death so Lazarus will chase you until he catches you and completes his orders." Lizzie hissed at Lazarus with her head tipped back and mouth wide open, baring rows of sharp fangs. Seeing all of her fangs exposed made me grateful that she was on my side.

Lazarus ignored the warning growls and stepped towards me. He opened his mouth to bare his fangs to me and it felt like looking into the jaws of my own death. Whether from Lazarus ripping my throat, or from a severe heart attack, I felt I was bound to die. Lazarus reached out to grab my shoulder.

I saw a flurry of movement in the corner of my eye as Lizzie sprung from the ceiling, landing on Lazarus's shoulders. "This ends now!" she shouted. She clamped her legs around his head and began scratching at his arms He was growling and thrashing to throw her off of him, but she was too strong for him to overpower. He reached up and behind to grab her shoulders to flip her over his head and to the ground, but Lizzie's legs stayed wrapped around his head so the two came crashing down together.

I hadn't seen anything like it since my childhood days of watching televised wrestling.

Lazarus maneuvered his giant frame so he was standing again, but he couldn't get Lizzie off of his shoulders. I could see the muscles in her thighs trembling as she squeezed his neck between them. Then, she reached forward to grab Lazarus's wrists, brought them together over his head, then pulled down and back. I watched her rip his arms off. I gasped; he let out a pitched cry like a wounded animal, then there was silence as his arms fell to the floor and turned to a small pile of ash.

Lizzie jumped off then faced the whimpering, armless giant. Lazarus fell to his knees in front of her. "It was a mistake to come here. Christo never should've sent you." She placed her hands on either side of his head and turned it slowly to the left as he gurgled. Then she snapped it to the right so fast that his head popped off his body. She held the shiny, bald head for half a second before letting it fall to the floor and roll next to the pile of ash that had formerly been his arms I saw the eyeballs roll back just before Lazarus's body collapsed with a generous thud. In a blink, he was gone — nothing more than a pile of ash. Lazarus Bedding would never harm us, or anyone else, ever again.

Lizzie walked over to me and put her hand on my shoulder as she asked, "Are you all right?"

"I'm fine, what about you? Did he hurt you?" I didn't — and couldn't — help her fight Lazarus, so would have felt terrible if she was hurt. "I'm all right. I'm much older and stronger than him so he wasn't going to get past me. But I'm sure Christo knew that. He probably sent him to scare you," she said.

Well, it worked... job well done.

"You were amazing against him, though," I said, feeling impressed by her tenacity and anxious to talk about something other than my fear.

"Thanks," she said off-handedly as she kicked the pile of Lazarus's ashes, sending particles into the air.

"What do we do now?" I asked. "Should I clean this up?"

Lizzie turned back to me and grabbed my hand as she announced, "Now, we go kill Christo."

We stood in the ash-covered kitchen, pieces of my front door splintered across every surface. She squeezed my hand as if to boost my confidence, which didn't really work. There was a sound behind us that reminded me of the nightly scratching from the rats that paraded the alley. Then a tiny tap at the kitchen window. But when I heard the voice from just outside the window, my stomach dropped.

"Guess who?"

I slowly turned to the window and saw Christo squatting on my fire escape. His face was low and near the glass, and his sinister smile widened as he scratched and tapped his long, sharp nails against the window.

Tap. Tap. Tap.

Scratch. Scratch. Scratch.

The steady beat of eerie noises was terrifying and hypnotic. "Go. Call. Paul," Lizzie said urgently, pulling me away from the window. I stood dumbstruck until she shouted next to my ear, "Now!"

I ran into the bedroom to look for my phone, hoping it'd

be in plain sight. I crashed around the room as I searched, and prayed. I rummaged through the dresser drawer, and knocked things off shelves, but couldn't lay hands on the cellphone. Damn! I saw my jeans crumpled in a heap at the foot of my bed and, flinging them onto a chair, saw the phone peeking out from under the bed.

Thank God.

I smashed the ON button with my trembling fingers. It seemed to take forever for the keypad to light up but with a cheerful *bloop* I heard the dial tone register and immediately punched in Paul's number.

Ring. Ring. Ring.

I heard the line pick up and Paul's voice answered, "Hey Ri—"

"It's Christo. He's here. In my apartment. And Lizzie already killed Lazarus." I whispered immediately and urgently.

"I'm on my way."

I threw the phone down on the bed and ran back to the kitchen, afraid of what I might find. But Lizzie was still standing in front of the window, staring at the monster just outside, waiting for him to make his move. He sneered at her.

"You can't have him," Lizzie said sternly.

Christo pulled the black leather jacket off his shoulders and slipped his arms out of the sleeves. "We'll see about that," he said smugly. It was like watching the devil himself threaten me in my own kitchen. "Try and stop me, Elizabeth, and I'll put you down as well." His words cut through me like a hot knife through butter.

Christo was toying with us. I watched him pick up a pebble from the ledge and casually toss it in his hand a few times. After three little tosses, he threw the rock through the window, shattering the glass into tiny shards. The pebble grazed the top of my shoulder and smashed into the fridge behind me, where it embedded in the metal door.

Fuck. Owwww. My shoulder was stinging where the pebble had buzzed me.

"You two had better duck," Christo laughed as he reached for more ammunition. "There are plenty more stones for me to throw." I saw he had a row of rocks on the ledge in front of him, and he grabbed one of the largest ones — it filled the palm of his massive hand. I tried to staunch the bleeding from my shoulder as he tossed the rock once to himself. He smiled right at me then whipped the rock at us through the shattered window, aiming for our heads. Lizzie and I both ducked. "Now, I'm coming in." He took his time standing up.

"Did you get a hold of Paul?" Lizzie whispered as we cowered on the floor. "We're going to need some help."

"He's on his way." I prayed that he'd make it to us in time.

"Okay, I'll hold him off until he gets here." Before I could react, Lizzie charged through the kitchen window using her vampire speed to stand directly in front of Christo on the fire escape, vampire to vampire. She took a swing at him. He ducked and then slammed her in the chest with both hands, sending her flying back into the apartment where she landed at my feet.

"Lizzie! Are — Are you all right?!" I shouted, fearing the worst.

She coughed once then said, "I'm fine," as she stood up. "We're just getting started."

I turned my attention back to the window where Christo was stepping one foot over the sill. He then smoothly stepped fully inside. The evil vampire had finally reached me and there was no stopping him; Christo was in my apartment. I immediately remembered, the one time Christo had visited me with Lazarus. It was a long time ago, but I had invited them both in and had, therefore, unwittingly given them the power to enter my apartment whenever they wished.

I... I have to do something. I need to do something!

"What you need to do, Rick, is get out of here!" Lizzie shouted.

"I'm not leaving you!" I turned to face Christo. I didn't care what he did to me, as long as he didn't hurt her. I stood as tall as I could, to show him I wasn't afraid, but my shaking hands betrayed the truth — I was deathly afraid.

"You can do what you want with me, just please don't hurt her." I was doing my best to negotiate with this killing machine. Christo reached out to grab my arm, then twisted it.

"Wow, Rick. How noble," he teased. "Stupid, but noble." He twisted my arm and wrenched my wrist, applying pressure so it hurt. "She's not worth it," Christo laughed as he insulted my Lizzie.

But then, from the belly of the building rose a deep, long howl. Christo's grip tightened around my arm just as a seven-foot werewolf walked through where my door used to be.

Triton! Thank God.

"Paul!" Lizzie shouted. Christo let go of me as he turned to the werewolf. I ran back to Lizzie still crouching on the floor, and stood over her.

The werewolf grabbed a dirty plate from the counter next to the sink and threw it directly at Christo's head with incredible force. He raised his arm swiftly to block it, sending the plate smashing into the wall causing it to shatter into nothing more than dust and tiny pieces. Christo stepped forward and pinned the werewolf's fur-matted arms to his side as he head-butted him with his brute strength. Triton went flying backwards and smashed into the wall where the force from the impact left a Triton-sized crater.

I was the only one left standing, so I did my best to stop him. I grabbed whatever was closest to me to use as a weapon, but it was just the mop. Rick Blume and his mop against Christo Daggen. I raised the handle high to whack against Christo's head, but he spun around in a flash and grabbed the mop with his left hand. He looked me in the eyes as he snapped the mop handle in two then said, "Tsk. Tsk. Tsk. That's not very nice, Rick."

Still holding half the mop over my head, he plunged the razor-sharp fingernails on his right hand into my stomach. I could feel the nails tearing through my flesh and pricking and slicing my organs. I was so shocked that I didn't feel anything. He slowly extracted his hand from my guts and I watched as my blood dripped from his hand and down to the floor, where it pooled on the linoleum.

"No, Christo! Please!" I heard Lizzie shout through the ringing that was filling my ears as I suddenly felt the pain in my belly register with my brain. I doubled-over, my arms clutching the gashes in my stomach, and felt my strength and energy immediately fade. I felt like I was dying. I fell forward and collapsed on the floor. Christo watched me fall and then crouched down to pat me on the shoulder. Through a devilish smile he hissed, "Good luck dying, friend."

Lizzie moved next to me and grabbed my hand. Her touch was cold, like always, but still very calming. I wanted her to save me, but all she did was hold my hand.

"Now to finish off the dog," Christo said, stepping over Lizzie and me. He grabbed Triton by the throat and lifted him high against the wall, choking him with all of his might. The werewolf's feet were off the ground and he was making guttural yelps as Christo squeezed the life from him. Triton was turning back into Paul as Christo was choking him.

There was movement in the hallway, then Maryanne's clear voice rang out, "That's enough of that!"

Before I could tell what was happening, Christo was flying across the room and crashed in a heap in the hallway. Paul crashed to the floor with Christo's sudden release. Maryanne waved her hands to knock Christo back again, his head smacking against the hallway wall with such force the floor rattled. Dead Laura stood right in front of Maryanne, as if to shield her from whatever this thousand-year-old monster was going to try to do to her.

"You bitch," he hissed from the rubble. "You Bogarden bitch — I should have killed you as soon as I learned you had any powers at all." Christo coughed once before he launched himself through one of my remaining unbroken windows. Amid the destruction, he shouted, "Get fucked, losers." Then he was gone. Just like that. One word from a Bogarden witch, had sent him running.

Lizzie was still holding my hand. I could feel her thumb brush against mine gently. I was face down on my stomach with my eyes closed as blood continued to pour from me. I was losing consciousness, but I could sense that she was near me.

"Rick, can you hear me?" She shook my shoulder carefully. I summoned the energy to open one eye for a moment — just long enough to see the tears running down her cheeks. "Please, handsome. Talk to me. I need you to tell me you're gonna make it, okay?"

I wanted to let her know that I was doing my best, that I wouldn't give in, but I was so tired and weak. And the pain was blinding. I was dying, but I accepted it with the hope that one of my talented friends would bring me back.

"Rick, please stay with me. I can't lose you. I... I... I love you." Lizzie's words cut deeper than Christo's nails. I tried to talk — I wanted to use my final breaths to tell her I love her. To tell her that she was everything to me. But I couldn't. I could barely breathe. The last thing I remember is hearing Lizzie shout to Maryanne, "I think he's dying. His pulse is really weak. Do something. Please!" Then, nothing. Everything was black, and I was gone.

***

After what seemed like years in a deep sleep, I heard Lizzie's voice again call out.

"Rick, can you hear me?" she asked, still holding my hand in hers. I had no sense of how much time had passed since I'd collapsed on the linoleum, but I felt different upon waking, since Christo had tried to kill me. I was no longer in any pain, but I felt incredibly weak and tired — I had no energy, and I was really hungry.

I opened my eyes to try to get my bearings and saw her. She was glowing, radiant. She was sitting next to me on the bed.

"I love you, too," I said. Lizzie telling me she loved me was the last thing I heard before blacking out and I felt compelled, driven to return her affection. I was happy, elated to see her, but she looked stricken and I knew immediately that something was wrong.

"What's wrong?" I asked, concerned. Was I dead, or alive? In Heaven, or Hell?

"It's your eyes," she said. "They're bright red."

Epilogue

Christo sat on the roof of an old abandoned church, perched like the stone gargoyle beside him. The rain continued to fall, running down his face and soaking his clothes. He jumped down from the rooftop and forced his way in the building from a third-story balcony. He landed in the room with a thud, crashing into a large piano and multiple chairs. He stood up, unharmed, and looked around the room. There were bookshelves on every wall, each one full of dusty books. A large, oversized mirror stood tall behind him, only partly covered by a sheet. He turned to stare at his reflection — which only he could see — and felt his age.

He remembered why he was there, and shook himself from his reverie to continue searching the disused room. He was looking for something he had hidden away over a hundred years ago — something only he knew about.

Except he couldn't remember where he'd put it. He began to throw and smash things as his frustration mounted. He was about to destroy everything in sight when he saw it peeking out from behind the piano he'd broken with his dramatic entrance: a very worn pine box covered by a sheet. He whipped the sheet off in a cloud of dust to inspect the makeshift casket. Christo placed both of his hands on the top of the box and then rested his head on it, ear against the wood.

"I can sense your soul. You are weak, but you're in there,"

he said with confidence.

Christo pried the nails from the top of the pine box with his talons and threw it aside to reveal a desiccated old man, bound by chains coiled around his hands and feet. Christo sneered then ripped the chains away, first from the hands, then from the feet.

Christo brought his own wrist to his mouth and pierced his leathery skin with his fangs. Blood began to stream out of him and he shoved his open wrist to the crinkled man's mouth.

"Drink," he said. "It's time for you to get up, old friend. It's time for you to help me, Richard."

CPSIA information can be obtained
at www.ICGtesting.com
Printed in the USA
BVHW092345020922
646137BV00002B/79

9 781804 392270